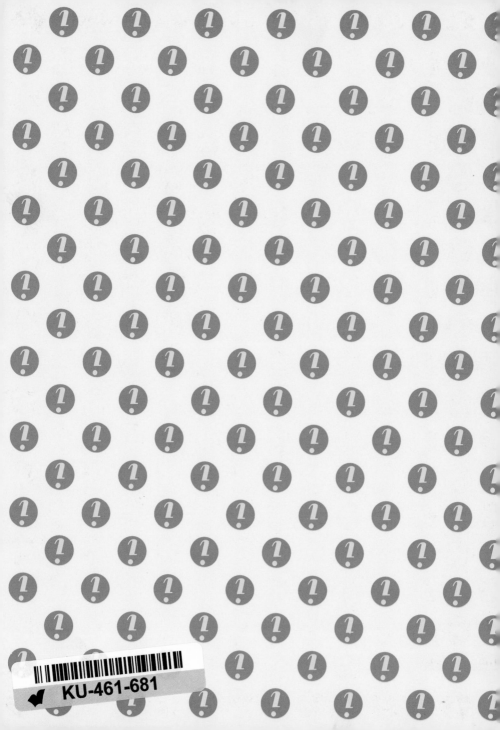

IDENTIFYING

i

ROCKS AND MINERALS

The new compact study guide and identifier

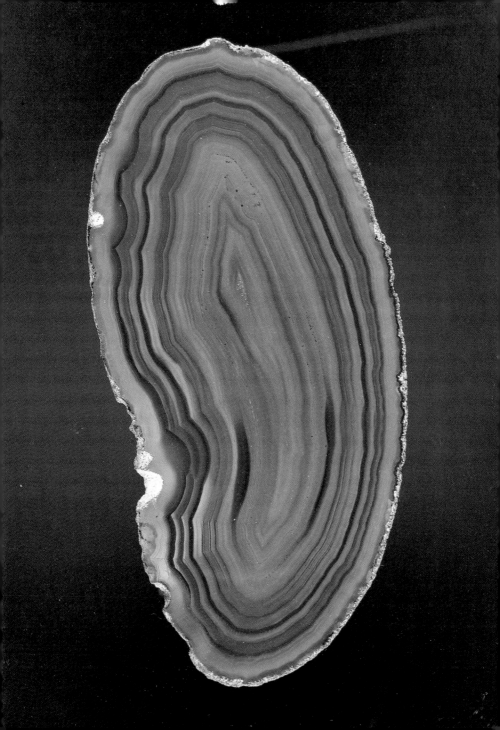

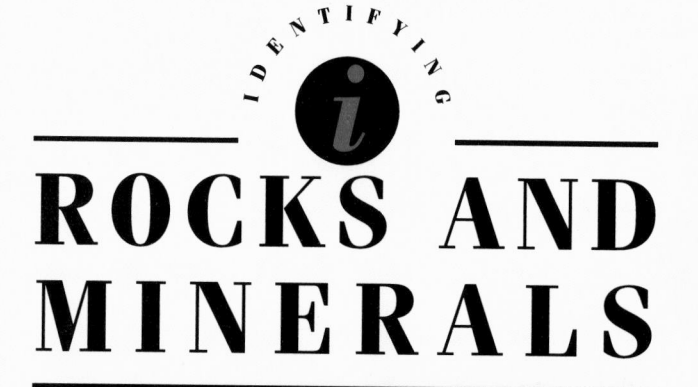

IDENTIFYING

ROCKS AND
MINERALS

The new compact study guide and identifier

Basil Booth

THE
APPLE
PRESS

A QUINTET BOOK

Published by The Apple Press
6 Blundell Street
London N7 9BH

ISBN 1-85076-450-6

This book was designed and produced by
Quintet Publishing Limited
6 Blundell Street
London N7 9BH

Project Editor: Laura Sandelson
Creative Director: Richard Dewing
Designer: Nicky Chapman
Editor: Michelle Clark

Typeset in Great Britain by
Central Southern Typesetters, Eastbourne
Manufactured in Singapore by
Eray Scan Pte. Ltd
Printed in Singapore by
Star Standard Industries Pte. Ltd

ACKNOWLEDGEMENT
The publishers would like to thank Geoscience Features
Picture Library for providing all the pictures used
in this book.

NOTE: For ease of use the names Czechoslovakia and
Yugoslavia have been retained to describe rocks and
minerals found in these regions. Information on the
distribution of rocks and minerals within the
new borders is not yet available.

CONTENTS

INTRODUCTION

This guide consists of two main parts which outline common features of minerals and rocks that differentiate them one from another. It is important to learn and understand these features in order to identify a particular rock or mineral accurately. The two parts each contain an introduction and identification profiles of important or interesting rocks and minerals.

To become a good geologist you need to see and handle as many different kinds of rocks and minerals as possible, so always take advantage of opportunities to visit museums to see collections of rocks and minerals and become familiar with them. Use this book to tell you more about them than the labels do and make a note of which ones you have seen.

Collecting specimens requires minimal equipment (see picture): a 1½ lb (0.7 kg) geological hammer, a 1-in (2.5-cm) rock chisel, narrow adhesive cloth tape (to write identification numbers on and stick these onto specimens), a pencil, a notebook (to record specimen details), collecting bags or old newspapers (in which to wrap your finds) and a stout bag or rucksack. Ordinary hammers and chisels are of little use as, unlike geological ones, they are not specially hardened.

A well-stoppered bottle of 40 per cent hydrochloric acid is also useful; it is used to identify calcite and limestones. Goggles, too, are a must for those who do not wear glasses (they stop rock splinters from entering the eyes when splitting rocks).

Specimens may be collected in quarries, on coastal cliffs, from building site and road excavations, etc, having gained permission to do so. When collecting in quarries and on cliffs remember to wear a hard hat; it could prevent a serious injury resulting from a dislodged stone. Also, always leave a note of your intended route before leaving, it could save time should an emergency arise. For this reason, too, it is always best to work in pairs, which

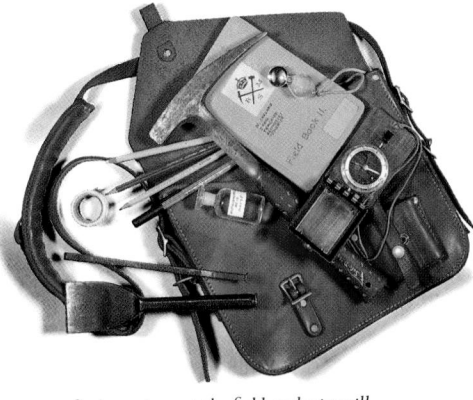

Basic equipment the field geologist will need for collecting specimens.

*Your rocks and minerals are best displayed
in a showcase with clear identification labels
accompanying each specimen.*

has the further advantage that two pairs of eyes are better than one when searching for specimens.

Not everyone has access to sites where many of the specimens described in this book are to be found naturally, but those who live in cities will generally be able to see many different types of rocks just walking down the street as they are often used to decorate buildings (granite, marble and lauvikite are the most commonly used). Further, as they are often highly polished, their minerals can be seen clearly.

When it comes to cleaning, soft rocks are best left alone, but harder ones can be cleaned with a small nylon brush and detergent. Minerals require more care and a small sable brush may be useful for this purpose. Remember not to wash soluble minerals such as rock salt. Also, some crystals are easily broken.

Once you have cleaned your specimens you will want to store or display them. A cabinet with shallow drawers that can be subdivided by means of small cardboard boxes is best for housing specimens, plus a name card giving location details. As your collection grows, however, you may wish to invest in an illuminated display cabinet to show off your best specimens.

MINERALS

....

MINERAL SHAPES

A mineral is produced by natural inorganic processes and has a composition that is either fixed or which varies within a definite range and an atomic structure that may be expressed in its crystalline form as well as other physical properties. It is these physical properties that enable minerals, and rocks, to be identified in the field.

A crystal is a regular polyhedral form, bounded by smooth surfaces, that a chemical compound assumes when it passes from its gaseous or liquid state to that of a solid. Under certain conditions – such as metamorphism – however, well-shaped crystals may grow within solid rock without having been through either a liquid or gaseous state. Remember that the crystal form of a mineral is an expression of its internal atomic structure and so is a valuable guide to its identification.

CRYSTAL SYSTEMS AND SYMMETRY

When a cube is held by its two opposite square faces it can be rotated so that a different square face will present itself four times (four-fold symmetry). Further examination of the cube will show that there are three such axes of four-fold

symmetry (written as 3iv). The cube has 13 symmetry axes – 3iv, 4iii, 6ii – but only the 3iv axis is characteristic of the cubic (or isometric) crystal system.

There are seven crystal systems, each based on the number of axes of symmetry developed. These are:

Cubic System: Three axes at 90 degrees, all equal in length

Tetragonal System: Three axes at 90 degrees, two of equal length, plus one longer axis

Orthorhombic System: Three axes at 90 degrees, all of different length

Monoclinic System: Two axes at 90 degrees, plus one axis at a different angle, all of different length

Triclinic System: Three axes of different length, none at 90 degrees

Hexagonal and Trigonal Systems: Three axes of equal length in one plane at 120 degrees, plus a longer axis at 90 degrees to the plane containing the other three (these two systems are distinguished by their differing symmetry – the hexagonal system has one six-fold symmetry and the trigonal has one three-fold symmetry).

Crystallographic axes are lines that intersect crystal faces. The cubic system has four such axes at 90 degrees to each

– CRYSTAL SYSTEMS AND SYMMETRY –

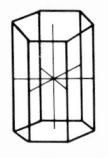

CUBIC SYSTEM

All three axes are the same length and are at right angles to each other.

TETRAGONAL SYSTEM

Three axes which are at right angles to each other. The two on the same plane are equal in length while the third is perpendicular to this plane.

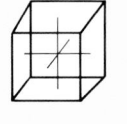

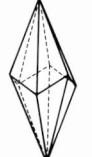

HEXAGONAL SYSTEM

Three of the four axes are in a single plane and radiate out equally from a central point. The fourth axis is at right angles to this plane and is unequal in length to the others. The crystal has one axis (long axis) of six fold symmetry.

TRIGONAL SYSTEM

There are three equal axes radiating from a single point in the same plane. A fourth axis is at right angles to this plane. The crystal has one axis of three fold symmetry.

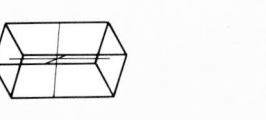

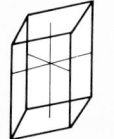

ORTHORHOMBIC SYSTEM

Three axes of unequal length set at right angles to one another.

MONOCLINIC SYSTEM

The prism has inclined top and bottom faces. There are three axes of unequal length: two are at right angles to each other with the third set at an incline to the plane of the other.

TRICLINIC SYSTEM

Three axes of unequal length set at three different angles to one another. Three pairs of faces.

other and the crystal faces that intersect these axes are identified by Millar indices – 100 for the cube face intersected by the A_1 axis, 010 for the face intersected by the A_2 axis and 001 for the face intersected by the A_3 axis. Where the A_1 axis intersects a face, the Millar index is 100; when all three axes intersect a crystal face, the Millar index is 111. A Millar index of 210 indicates that the A_1 axis cuts the face at a different distance to that of the A_2 axis.

All axes are divided into positive and negative portions which start at the point of intersection – or origin – of the axes. The negative axis is represented by a bar above the index (eg $10\bar{1}$); the positive portion of the axis has no bar (eg 101).

Related to the crystal structure is a property called the cleavage. Planes of weakness in the crystal lattice reveal themselves in the tendency for the crystal to split in a certain direction, eg mica, in which the silicate molecules are arranged in flat sheets, can flake away like the leaves of a book.

A crystal may grow in two different directions from one face. The result is called a twin. Twinned crystals can be recognized by the presence of re-entrant angles – something not found in single crystals. Commonly, twinning occurs in the cubic system, where one cube penetrates another (eg pyrites and fluorite).

MINERAL IDENTIFICATION

Minerals are identified in the field on the basis of the following properties:

LIGHT

Some colours are striking and serve a diagnostic purpose, while others are of lesser

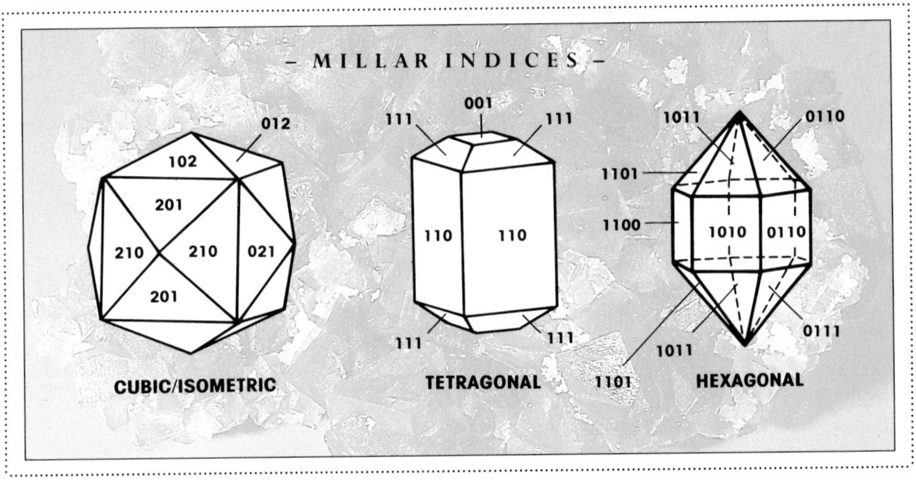

– MILLAR INDICES –

CUBIC/ISOMETRIC   TETRAGONAL   HEXAGONAL

value. The colours of the following minerals help identify them:

Malachite – green
Pyrites – brassy yellow
Galena – lead grey

The colours of the following are variable and so are of less diagnostic value:

Fluorspar
Barytes
Quartz

LUSTRE

Lustre is the light reflected off the surface of a mineral in a characteristic way. It can take several forms:

Metallic like polished metal, eg pyrites

Pyrites (iron sulphide) displays brilliant metallic lustre.

Adamantine brilliant, like diamonds, eg cassiterite
Vitreous like broken glass, eg quartz
Resinous like resin or wax, eg sphalerite
Pearly like pearls, eg stilbite
Silky like silk, eg satin spa
Splendent brilliant reflectivity, eg specularite

Shining reflects an image, but not clearly, eg selenite
Glistening reflects light, but not an image, eg chalcopyrite
Glimmering imperfect reflections from points on specimen, eg flint

STREAK

The streak is the colour the mineral is when it is powdered. You can either crush a small piece of the mineral or draw the mineral across a piece of unglazed porcelain – a streak plate. This means of identification is valuable for:

Azurite, which is pale blue
Haematite, which is reddish-brown
Sphalerite, which is pale brownish-yellow
Malachite, which is pale green
Native copper, which is grey
Chalcopyrite, which is greenish-black

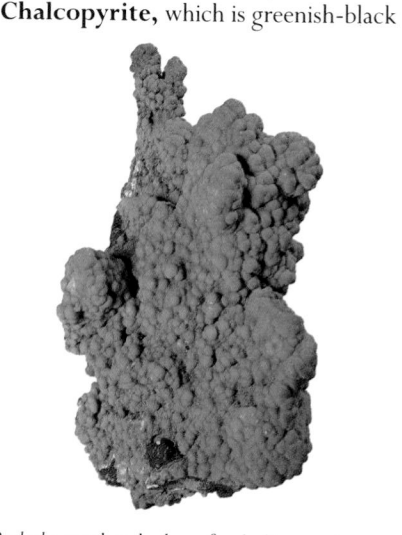

Both the streak and colour of malachite are the same.

TRANSPARENCY

There are different degrees of transparency. Minerals are **transparent** when the outline of objects can be seen clearly through the specimen. **Semitransparent** minerals are those where objects are indistinct when seen through the specimen, while **translucent** ones are those where light passes through the specimen, but it cannot be seen through. **Opaque** minerals are those where no light can be seen through them.

FRACTURE

When a specimen breaks smoothly and evenly along certain planes, these are called cleavage planes and are numbered using Millar Indices. Other specimens break randomly, while some may give a distinctive type of break or fracture:

Conchoidal breaks with concentric cavities, eg quartz

Subconchoidal indistinct conchoidal, eg tourmaline

Even surface flat, but slightly rough, eg barytes

Uneven surface rough and irregular, eg pyroxene

Hackly surface has sharp points, eg specularite

Earthy surface dull and crumbly, eg limonite

HARDNESS

Also tested is the hardness of the mineral – its resistance to abrasion. Most minerals have a specific hardness, though in some

A selection of native diamond crystals. Diamond, the crystalline form of carbon, is the hardest substance known.

Scale	Comparison	Mineral test
1	TALC	Powdered by finger nail
2	GYPSUM	Scratched by finger nail
3	CALCITE	Scratched by copper coin
4	FLUORSPAR	Easily scratched by pocket knife
5	APATITE	Just scratched by pocket knife
6	ORTHOCLASE	Scratched by steel file
7	QUARTZ	Scratches glass window
8	TOPAZ	Easily scratches quartz
9	CORUNDUM	Easily scratches topaz
10	DIAMOND	Hardest known substance, cannot be scratched

it may vary slightly. The hardness is determined by rubbing the unknown mineral with a known reference mineral from Mohs' scale of hardness. If the unknown is, say, scratched by quartz but not by apatite, then the hardness is 6.

Mohs' set of hardness can be purchased at most mineralogists or you can build up your own. Obviously, though, do not spoil a good crystal by scratching its faces.

TENACITY

Another related test is for tenacity. Minerals are termed:

Sectile if they are easily cut by a knife, eg gypsum

Brittle if they crumble when hit by a hammer, eg calcite

Malleable if cut slices can be flattened by hitting them with a hammer, eg copper

Flexible if they will bend without breaking, eg chrysotile

SPECIFIC GRAVITY

This is the weight of a mineral compared with the weight of an equal volume of water. Anything with a Specific Gravity of more than 3, eg fluorite, would be noticeable and something like Galena, with a Specific Gravity of 7.6, would be very obvious.

Galena not only has a high specific gravity, but it is also very brittle.

– **HOW TO USE THIS BOOK** –

Below each identifier entry is a group of symbols that indicate the hardness, specific gravity and crystal system (or classification). The symbols to indicate the different systems are as follows:

MOHS' HARDNESS

SPECIFIC GRAVITY

TETRAGONAL

HEXAGONAL

CUBIC

TRIGONAL

AMORPHOUS

ORTHORHOMBIC

MONOCLINIC

TRICLINIC

MINERAL IDENTIFIER

GOLD Au
NATIVE METAL AND NON-METAL GROUP

DISTINCTIVE FEATURES Malleability, colour, association with pyrites, galena and chalcopyrite.

COLOUR Deep gold-yellow to pale yellow.

LUSTRE Metallic.

STREAK Golden-yellow to reddish.

TRANSPARENCY Opaque.

CLEAVAGE None.

FRACTURE Hackly.

TENACITY Ductile, malleable.

FORMS Flat plates, arborescent, crystals rare.

TWINNING On 111.

VARIETIES Usually alloyed with silver: ordinary gold is 10 per cent silver, electrum is 38 per cent silver and is, therefore, a pale yellow to silvery colour, while other varieties contain up to 20 per cent copper and palladium.

USES Monetary standard, jewellery, electronics, aircraft window screening.

OCCURRENCE Worldwide, mostly in quartz veins and placer deposits, although it does occur in igneous, metamorphic and sedimentary rocks, but particularly Ural Mountains, Siberia, Alps, India, China, New Zealand, Queensland, South Africa (Transvaal), Colombia, Mexico, Yukon, USA (along mountain ranges in western states).

MOHS' HARDNESS: 2.5–3

SPECIFIC GRAVITY: 15.6–19.33, pure form

CRYSTAL SYSTEM: Cubic

SILVER Ag
NATIVE METAL AND NON-METAL GROUP

DISTINCTIVE FEATURES Malleability, colour and specific gravity.

COLOUR Silvery white.

LUSTRE Metallic.

STREAK Silvery white.

TRANSPARENCY Opaque.

CLEAVAGE None.

FRACTURE Hackly.

TENACITY Ductile, malleable.

FORMS Distorted crystals, reticulated and arborescent.

TWINNING None.

VARIETIES Usually alloyed with gold or copper.

USES Coinage, jewellery, ornaments, electronics.

OCCURRENCE Native silver is rare and is often associated with silver minerals. Norway, Central Europe, Australia (New South Wales), Chile, Mexico, USA (Michigan, Montana, Idaho, Colorado), Canada (Ontario).

MOHS' HARDNESS: 2.5–3

SPECIFIC GRAVITY: 10.10–10.50, pure form

CRYSTAL SYSTEM: Cubic

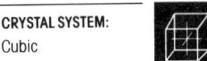

COPPER Cu

NATIVE METAL AND NON-METAL GROUP

DISTINCTIVE FEATURES Colour, malleability, ductility, association with malachite and other copper ores. Dissolves in nitric acid, producing red nitrous fumes (care is needed for this test).

COLOUR Copper-red.

LUSTRE Metallic.

STREAK Metallic, coppery, shining.

TRANSPARENCY Opaque.

CLEAVAGE None.

FRACTURE Hackly.

TENACITY Ductile, malleable.

FORMS Twisted, wirelike, platy, crystals uncommon.

TWINNING On 111.

VARIETIES Veins, strings, sheets, crystal masses.

USES Electrical conductor in wires, electronics, alloyed with tin – to produce bronze – and zinc – to produce brass.

OCCURRENCE Native copper is usually of secondary origin in copper ore veins, sandstone, limestone, slate and near igneous rocks. Russia, south-west UK, Australia (New South Wales), Bolivia, Mexico, USA (Lake Superior area, Arizona, New Mexico).

MOHS' HARDNESS: 2.5–3.00	SPECIFIC GRAVITY: 8.8–8.9	CRYSTAL SYSTEM: Cubic

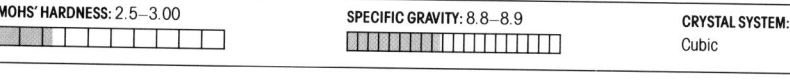

SULPHUR s

NATIVE METAL AND NON-METAL GROUP

DISTINCTIVE FEATURES Yellow colour, melts and burns readily with blue flame, giving off choking sulphur dioxide fumes. Often contaminated with clay or bitumen.

COLOUR Bright yellow to red or yellow-grey.

LUSTRE Resinous.

STREAK White.

TRANSPARENCY Transparent to transluscent.

CLEAVAGE On 001, 110, 111.

FRACTURE Conchoidal to sectile.

TENACITY Ductile when heated.

FORMS Pyramidal to tabular.

TWINNING Rare.

VARIETIES None.

USES Making sulphuric acid, gunpowder, fireworks, insecticides and fungicides, vulcanizing rubber, medicines.

OCCURRENCE Mostly in young sedimentary rocks, often clays, associated with bitumen. Frequently as small crystals around fumaroles on volcanoes. Sicily (large crystals, associated with selenite and calcite), USA (mainly in Louisiana and Texas, but also found around fumaroles in Yellowstone Park, Sulphur Bank mercury mine in California and in many other states).

MOHS' HARDNESS: 1.5–2.5	SPECIFIC GRAVITY: 2.05–2.09	CRYSTAL SYSTEM: Orthorhombic

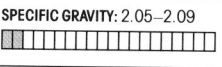
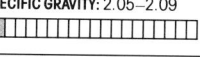

DIAMOND c
NATIVE METAL AND NON-METAL GROUP

DISTINCTIVE FEATURES Brilliant lustre and extreme hardness.
COLOUR Colourless, white or, rarely, yellow, orange, blue or green.
LUSTRE Adamantine to greasy.
STREAK None.
TRANSPARENCY Transparent, but may be translucent to opaque.
CLEAVAGE Perfect on 111.
FRACTURE Conchoidal.
TENACITY Not applicable.
FORMS Octahedral and more complex crystals; also spherical and massive.
TWINNING Common on 111.
VARIETIES None.
USES Gemstone, abrasive, cutting tools and drill bits, polishing gemstones.

OCCURRENCE Mainly in alluvial gravels, clay and kimberlite (a type of peridotite formed under high pressure). Largest found was the Cullinan, at 3025 carats and a little over 1 lb 5 oz (0.6 kg). It has since been cut into 105 stones, including the largest cut stone currently in existence at 516 carats. South Africa, India, Urals, USA (Georgia and Carolina).

MOHS' HARDNESS: 10 – hardest substance known

SPECIFIC GRAVITY: 3.516–3.525

CRYSTAL SYSTEM: Cubic

GRAPHITE c
NATIVE METAL AND NON-METAL GROUP

DISTINCTIVE FEATURES Silvery black colour with pencil black streak. Very soft with greasy feel. Extremely dirty to handle.
COLOUR Steel black to grey.
LUSTRE Metallic, dull, earthy.
STREAK Black.
TRANSPARENCY Opaque.
CLEAVAGE Perfect basal.
FRACTURE Rough when not on cleavage.
TENACITY Not applicable.
FORMS Tabular crystals – six-sided, foliated masses, granular to compact masses.
TWINNING None.
VARIETIES None.

USES 'Lead' in pencils, graphite lubricants, paints, high temperature crucibles, electrodes.
OCCURRENCE In gneiss, schists, limestones and quartzites. Siberian gneisses, Ceylon granulites, Finnish limestones, Mexico, USA (Adirondack quartzites and gneisses, Rhode Island limestones, Pennsylvania, Montana and New Mexico).

MOHS' HARDNESS: 1.0–2.0

SPECIFIC GRAVITY: 2.09–2.23

CRYSTAL SYSTEM: Trigonal

CORUNDUM Al_2O_3
OXIDE GROUP

DISTINCTIVE FEATURES Hardness, form, association with crystalline rocks and gneisses.

COLOUR Variable: the common form is brown to grey, but it can also be white, red, blue and various shades of yellow.

LUSTRE Adamantine to vitreous.

STREAK Same as colour – usually white.

TRANSPARENCY Transparent to translucent to opaque.

CLEAVAGE Occasionally parts on 0001.

FRACTURE Generally uneven, but sometimes conchoidal.

TENACITY Brittle.

FORMS Barrel-shaped hexagonal, rhombic crystals often truncated on 0001.

TWINNING On $10\bar{1}1$; occasionally interpenetrant.

VARIETIES Sapphire, which is blue, ruby, which is red, oriental topaz, which is yellow, oriental amethyst, which is purple, dull or opaque varieties of the mineral and emery, which is a granular corundum with magnetite and ilmenite.

USES Gemstones, when transparent, abrasives and grinding powders.

OCCURRENCE In crystalline rocks, schists, gneisses. Burma, Cambodia, India, Japan, the Urals in Russia, Switzerland, Greece, Madagascar, South Africa, USA (New York, New Jersey, Pennsylvania, Carolina, Georgia, Montana), Canada (Ontario).

MOHS' HARDNESS: 9

SPECIFIC GRAVITY: 3.95–4.10

CRYSTAL SYSTEM:
Hexagonal
(rhombohedral)

– VARIETIES –

Ruby

Sapphire

HAEMATITE Fe₂O₃
OXIDE GROUP

DISTINCTIVE FEATURES Streak, colour, form, density.
COLOUR Metallic grey to earthy red.
LUSTRE Metallic to splendent.
STREAK Bright red to Indian red.
TRANSPARENCY Opaque.
CLEAVAGE None.
FRACTURE Uneven to subconchoidal.
TENACITY Brittle, but elastic in thin plates.
FORMS Tabular to thick crystals.
TWINNING Interpenetrant on 0001 and 01$\bar{1}$2.
VARIETIES Specularite, which has splendent tabular crystals, often in brilliant masses, pencil ore, which is a fibrous compact form, often used in jewellery, kidney ore, which has botryoidal masses resembling kidneys, clay iron-stone, which has deep red-brown compact masses, often in sedimentary rocks.
USES Principal ore of iron.
OCCURRENCE Ubiquitous in formation and occurrence. The Urals in Russia, Romania, Austria, Germany, Switzerland, France, Italy, UK, Ascension Island, Brazil, USA (Michigan, Wisconsin, Minnesota, Wyoming, New York, Colorado), Canada (Nova Scotia, Newfoundland).

MOHS' HARDNESS: 5.5–6.5

SPECIFIC GRAVITY: 4.9–5.3

CRYSTAL SYSTEM: Hexagonal **(rhombohedral)**

SPINEL MgAl₂O₄ to MgO.Al₂O₃
OXIDE GROUP

DISTINCTIVE FEATURES Small octahedral crystals that are usually deep red, but can be varying shades of yellow, blue or green.
COLOUR Variable – mostly red, but yellow, blue, green, brown and black forms occur.
LUSTRE Vitreous.
STREAK White.
TRANSPARENCY Transparent to translucent.
CLEAVAGE Poor on 111.
FRACTURE Conchoidal, but difficult to see.
TENACITY Brittle.
FORMS Octahedral, sometimes rounded. Cubes rare.
TWINNING Common on 111.
VARIETIES Ruby spinel, which is medium red, pleonast, which is deep green to brown or black and chrome spinel, which is green to dark yellow.
USES Transparent crystals of excellent colour are used as gemstones.
OCCURRENCE In gem gravels associated with ruby and limestones and basic igneous rocks, such as peridotite. Ceylon, Burma, Italy, Sweden, Madagascar, USA (New York, New Jersey, North Carolina), Canada (Ontario, Quebec, Ottawa).

MOHS' HARDNESS: 8.0

SPECIFIC GRAVITY: 3.5–4.0

CRYSTAL SYSTEM: Cubic

MAGNETITE Fe''Fe'''₂O₄. to FeO.Fe₂O₃
OXIDE GROUP

DISTINCTIVE FEATURES Heavy and magnetic, often with North and South poles.
COLOUR Black.
LUSTRE Metallic.
STREAK Black.
TRANSPARENCY Opaque.
CLEAVAGE Indistinct.
FRACTURE Uneven.
TENACITY Brittle.
FORMS Octahedral, massive to fine granular.
TWINNING On 111.
VARIETIES Lodestone, which is strongly magnetic and has North and South poles.
USES Iron ore.

OCCURRENCE Found in most igneous rocks, particularly those of basic composition, black beach sands, serpentines and metamorphic rocks. Sweden and Norway (largest deposits in the world), Siberia, Australia, Europe, Brazil, USA (New York, New Jersey, Pennsylvania, Arkansas, Utah), Cuba, Canada (Ontario, Quebec).

MOHS' HARDNESS: 5.5–6.5 | **SPECIFIC GRAVITY:** 5.17–5.18 | **CRYSTAL SYSTEM:** Cubic

CHROMITE FeCr₂O₄ to FeO.Cr₂O₃
OXIDE GROUP

DISTINCTIVE FEATURES Streak, feebly magnetic.
COLOUR Black.
LUSTRE Submetallic.
STREAK Brown.
TRANSPARENCY Opaque.
CLEAVAGE None.
FRACTURE Uneven to rough.
TENACITY Brittle.
FORMS Octahedral. Massive to granular.
TWINNING None.
VARIETIES None.
USES Chromium ore, for hardening steel, chrome plating and chromium pigments.

OCCURRENCE In peridotites and serpentine and often associated with magnetite. The Urals, Austria, Germany, France, UK, South Africa, Iran, USA (New Jersey, Pennsylvania, North Carolina, California), Canada (Newfoundland).

MOHS' HARDNESS: 5.5 | **SPECIFIC GRAVITY:** 4.1–4.9 | **CRYSTAL SYSTEM:** Cubic

RUTILE TiO₂
OXIDE GROUP

DISTINCTIVE FEATURES Bright metallic coppery to reddish-brown needle-like crystals in quartz crystals or as darker, compact masses in acid to intermediate crystalline rocks. Sometimes in limestones, where deposited by mineralizing fluids. Transparent varieties have adamantine lustre, but many specimens are opaque. Produces a pale brown streak.

COLOUR Coppery to reddish-brown.

LUSTRE Metallic to adamantine.

STREAK Pale brown.

TRANSPARENCY Transparent to opaque.

CLEAVAGE On 110 and 100.

FRACTURE Subconchoidal to uneven.

TENACITY Brittle.

FORMS Often found as prismatic acicular crystals in quartz. Occasionally compact to massive.

TWINNING On 101, sometimes with complex geniculation.

VARIETIES Ordinary rutile is brown-red to black, iron-rich rutile is black, while chromium-rich rutile is green.

USES Ore of titanium and manufacture of items where strength is of great importance.

OCCURRENCE In acid to intermediate crystalline rocks. Austria, Switzerland, France, Norway, Australia, Brazil, USA (Vermont, Massachusetts, Connecticut, New York, Virginia, Georgia, Carolina, Arkansas).

MOHS' HARDNESS: 6.0–6.5	SPECIFIC GRAVITY: 4.18–4.25	CRYSTAL SYSTEM: Tetragonal

PYROLUSITE MnO₂
OXIDE GROUP

DISTINCTIVE FEATURES Hardness and colour of streak.

COLOUR Iron black to dark steel grey; occasionally bluish.

LUSTRE Metallic.

STREAK Same as colour.

TRANSPARENCY Opaque.

CLEAVAGE On 100 and 011.

FRACTURE Rough.

TENACITY Brittle.

FORMS Commonly dendritic, granular to massive.

TWINNING None.

VARIETIES Crystals, massive and the very pure form, which is called polianite.

USES Ore of manganese, for colouring glass, in the preparation of chlorine, bromine and oxygen.

OCCURRENCE Concentrated as a secondary ore deposit by circulating fluids, often in clays and siltstones. Brazil, Cuba, Germany, India, the Urals, USA (Arkansas, Georgia, Virginia, Minnesota, Tennessee and lesser amounts in other states).

MOHS' HARDNESS: 2.0–2.5	SPECIFIC GRAVITY: 4.73–4.86	CRYSTAL SYSTEM: Orthorhombic

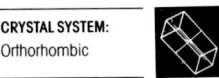

CASSITERITE SnO₂.1
OXIDE GROUP

DISTINCTIVE FEATURES Hardness, colour, form and specific gravity.
COLOUR Brown to black.
LUSTRE Brilliant.
STREAK White to brownish.
TRANSPARENCY Nearly transparent to opaque.
CLEAVAGE Poor on 100.
FRACTURE Subconchoidal to rough.
TENACITY Brittle.
FORMS Dumpy pyramids and prismatic.
TWINNING Interpenetrant, often on 101. Also elbow twins.

VARIETIES Tin stone, which is crystalline and massive, wood tin, which is botryoidal and reniform with a fibrous structure, toad's eye, which is the same as wood tin, but on a smaller scale, and stream tin, which is cassiterite in the form of sand, admixed with other mineral and rock grains.
USES Principal ore of tin.
OCCURRENCE Mostly in granitic rocks and associated pegmatites. Often associated with fluorite, apatite, topaz and wolframite deposited by mineralizing fluids. Malaysia, Indonesia, Bolivia, Congo, Mexico, England, Eastern Europe, USA (California, South Carolina, South Dakota, New Hampshire, Maine, New Mexico, Texas).

MOHS' HARDNESS: 6–7	SPECIFIC GRAVITY: 6.4–7.1	CRYSTAL SYSTEM: Tetragonal

BAUXITE Al₂O₃.2H₂O
HYDROXIDE GROUP

DISTINCTIVE FEATURES Massive, red to reddish-yellow, earthy and amorphous.
COLOUR Shades of red to yellow, occasionally white.
LUSTRE Earthy.
STREAK Reddish.
TRANSPARENCY Opaque.
CLEAVAGE None.
FRACTURE Earthy.
TENACITY Not applicable.
FORMS Mostly in reddish, earthy-like masses, but sometimes occurs as fine grains.
TWINNING None.
VARIETIES Concretions of grains, clay or earthy-like masses.

USES Principally ore of aluminium and in ceramics.
OCCURRENCE Formed by weathering of aluminium rocks under tropical conditions and deposited as a colloid. France, Germany, Romania, Italy, Venezuela, USA (Arkansas, Georgia, Alabama, Missouri).

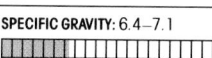

MOHS' HARDNESS: Not applicable	SPECIFIC GRAVITY: 2.5	CRYSTAL SYSTEM: Colloidal or amorphous

LIMONITE $2Fe_2O_3.3H_2O$
HYDROXIDE GROUP

DISTINCTIVE FEATURES Ochreous yellow, earthy, amorphous.
COLOUR Deep ochreous yellow to brown and black.
LUSTRE Earthy, dull.
STREAK Ochreous yellow.
TRANSPARENCY Opaque.
CLEAVAGE None.
FRACTURE Earthy.
TENACITY Not applicable.
FORMS Compact to stalactitic and botryoidal ochreous earthy masses.
TWINNING None.

VARIETIES Bog ore, which occurs in bogs where it petrifies plant material, clay-ironstone, which has concretions and nodules and is mostly found in sandstone rocks.
USES Pigments and iron ore.
OCCURRENCE Deposited near the surface after weathering of iron-rich minerals. Worldwide, but particularly in Canada (Nova Scotia), USA (ubiquitous).

MOHS' HARDNESS: 5.0—5.5

SPECIFIC GRAVITY: 3.5—4.0

CRYSTAL SYSTEM:
Amorphous

ORPIMENT As_2S_3
SULPHIDE GROUP

DISTINCTIVE FEATURES Lemon yellow, often tinged with fine streaks of orange, its lustre and flexibility in thin plates. When heated in a closed tube, it yields a dark red liquid that becomes yellow when cold.
Note: Arsenic trisulphide is poisonous.
COLOUR Lemon yellow to medium yellow.

LUSTRE Pearly to resinous.
STREAK Slightly paler than colour.
TRANSPARENCY Subtransparent to translucent.
CLEAVAGE Perfect on 010 and striated.
FRACTURE Rough.
TENACITY Sectile.
FORMS Massive and foliated, but the tiny crystals are difficult to see.

TWINNING None.
VARIETIES None.
USES Pigment and for removing hair from animal skins.
OCCURRENCE Often associated with the equally poisonous orange-red realgar, arsenic sulphide. "Czechoslovakia", Romania, Japan, USA (Utah, Nevada, Yellowstone Park).

MOHS' HARDNESS: 1.5—2

SPECIFIC GRAVITY: 3.4—3.5

CRYSTAL SYSTEM:
Monoclinic

CINNABAR HgS
SULPHIDE GROUP

DISTINCTIVE FEATURES Colour and streak, high specific gravity and its softness. When heated in a tube it yields globules of mercury metal which settle on the sides of the tube.

COLOUR Cochineal red to brownish-red.

LUSTRE Adamantine to dull.

STREAK Scarlet.

TRANSPARENCY Transparent to opaque.

CLEAVAGE Perfect on 10$\bar{1}$0.

FRACTURE Uneven to subconchoidal.

TENACITY Not applicable.

FORMS Rhombohedral to tabular in habit. Also granular and massive.

TWINNING Interpenetrant.

VARIETIES None.

USES Only common, and therefore principal, ore of mercury.

OCCURRENCE Russia, "Yugoslavia" (near Belgrade), "Czechoslovakia", Bavaria (good crystals), Italy, Spain, Peru, China, USA (California, Nevada, Utah, Oregon).

MOHS' HARDNESS: 2.0–2.5

SPECIFIC GRAVITY: 8.0–8.2

CRYSTAL SYSTEM: Hexagonal (trigonal)

STIBNITE Sb₂S₃
SULPHIDE GROUP

DISTINCTIVE FEATURES Colour, softness, cleavage. Also, when heated in a tube, it yields sulphur dioxide and fumes of antimony oxide, the latter condensing to form a white powder.

COLOUR Steel grey to dull grey, often with a black, iridescent tarnish.

LUSTRE Metallic; splendent on fresh crystal surfaces.

STREAK Same as colour.

TRANSPARENCY Opaque.

CLEAVAGE Perfect on 010, less so on 001.

FRACTURE Small-scale subconchoidal.

TENACITY Somewhat sectile.

FORMS Masses of radiating elongated crystals. Also massive and granular.

TWINNING None.

VARIETIES Metastibnite, which is an earthy, reddish deposit found at Steamboat Springs, Nevada in USA.

USES Principal source of antimony.

OCCURRENCE Mostly in quartz veins in granites, but also in schists and limestones. China, Algeria, Mexico, Germany, Romania, Italy, Borneo, Peru, USA (California, Nevada – scarce in both states).

MOHS' HARDNESS: 2.0

SPECIFIC GRAVITY: 4.562–4.62

CRYSTAL SYSTEM: Orthorhombic

MOLYBDENITE MoS₂
SULPHIDE GROUP

DISTINCTIVE FEATURES Soft, flexible, silvery, foliated scales and has a greasy feel. When heated in a tube, it yields sulphurous fumes and a pale yellow sublimate.
COLOUR Silvery lead grey.
LUSTRE Metallic.
STREAK Grey to greenish-grey.

TRANSPARENCY Opaque.
CLEAVAGE Perfect basal on 0001.
FRACTURE Not applicable.
TENACITY Flexible, but not elastic.
FORMS Tabular prisms, often short and tapering and often foliated or massive.
TWINNING None.
VARIETIES None.

USES Principal ore of molybdenum.
OCCURRENCE In granite pegmatites and quartz veins, also in syenites and gneisses. Norway, UK, Australia (Queensland), Namibia, USA (New Hampshire, Connecticut, Pennsylvania, Washington).

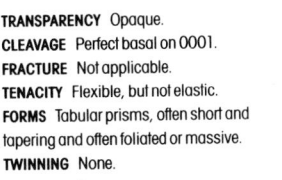

MOHS' HARDNESS: 1.0–1.5

SPECIFIC GRAVITY: 4.7–4.8

CRYSTAL SYSTEM: Hexagonal

GALENA PbS
SULPHIDE GROUP

DISTINCTIVE FEATURES Cubic, cleavage, colour, high specific gravity.
COLOUR Lead grey, often silvery.
LUSTRE Metallic, shining.
STREAK Lead grey.
TRANSPARENCY Opaque.
CLEAVAGE Perfect on 100, 010 and 001.
FRACTURE Flat on cubic form to even.
TENACITY Not applicable.
FORMS Mainly cubes, tabular, sometimes skeletal crystals.
TWINNING On 111, interpenetrant and contact twins common.
VARIETIES None.
USES Chief ore of lead and important source of silver.

OCCURRENCE Widespread in beds and veins due to hydrothermal action of mineralizing fluids. Found in limestones, dolomites, granites and other crystalline rocks and is often associated with sphalerite, pyrite, calcite and quartz. France, Austria, UK, Australia, Chile, Peru, USA (extensive deposits in Missouri, Illinois and Iowa and also found in lesser quantities in many other states).

MOHS' HARDNESS: 2.5–2.75

SPECIFIC GRAVITY: 7.4–7.6

CRYSTAL SYSTEM: Cubic

SPHALERITE ZnS
SULPHIDE GROUP

DISTINCTIVE FEATURES Resinous lustre and colour and often associated with galena, pyrite, quartz, calcite, barytes and fluorite.

COLOUR Dull yellow-brown to black, also greenish to white, but nearly colourless when pure.

LUSTRE Resinous and adamantine.

STREAK Pale brown to light yellow.

TRANSPARENCY Transparent to translucent.

CLEAVAGE Perfect on 110.

FRACTURE Conchoidal.

TENACITY Not applicable.

FORMS Dodecahedra, massive to granular, sometimes amorphous.

TWINNING Common on 111.

VARIETIES None.

USES Principal ore of zinc.

OCCURRENCE Can occur in veins in most rocks, where it is associated with galena, pyrite, quartz and calcite. Romania, Italy (Tuscany), Switzerland, Spain, UK, Sweden, Mexico, Canada, USA (Missouri, Colorado, Montana, Wisconsin, Idaho and Kansas).

Sphalerite on galena

MOHS' HARDNESS: 3.5–4.0

SPECIFIC GRAVITY: 3.9–4.1

CRYSTAL SYSTEM:
Cubic

CHALCOPYRITE CuFeS₂
SULPHIDE GROUP

DISTINCTIVE FEATURES Similar to pyrite but deeper in colour and often iridescent. Usually massive, brittle and soluble in nitric acid.

COLOUR Tarnished brassy gold, often iridescent.

LUSTRE Metallic.

STREAK Green-black.

TRANSPARENCY Opaque.

CLEAVAGE Variable on 201.

FRACTURE Uneven.

TENACITY Not applicable.

FORMS Usually massive, sometimes rounded. Crystals less common than for pyrites.

TWINNING On 111 or 101.

VARIETIES None.

USES Principal ore of copper.

OCCURRENCE Metalliferous veins in granites, gneisses and schists. Often associated with bornite, malachite, azurite and quartz. Germany, Italy, France, UK, Spain, Sweden, South America, Australasia, USA (New York, Pennsylvania, Missouri, Colorado), Namibia.

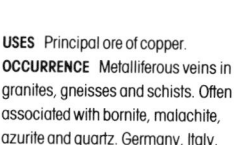

MOHS' HARDNESS: 3.5–4.0

SPECIFIC GRAVITY: 4.1–4.3

CRYSTAL SYSTEM:
Cubic

P Y R I T E FeS₂
SULPHIDE GROUP

DISTINCTIVE FEATURES Glistening to metallic brassy gold cubic and pyritohedron crystals and produces a greenish-black streak.
COLOUR Pale brassy gold.
LUSTRE Metallic to glistening.
STREAK Greenish-black to brown-black.
TRANSPARENCY Opaque.
CLEAVAGE Poor on 100 and 111.
FRACTURE Usually uneven, sometimes conchoidal.
TENACITY Not applicable.
FORMS Cubes, pyritohedrons. Often intergrown, massive, radiated, granular, globular and stalactitic.
TWINNING Interpenetrant twins common on 110.

VARIETIES. None.
USES As source of gold and copper, which it contains in small amounts. Also to produce sulphur, sulphuric acid and iron sulphate.
OCCURRENCE Universal – the most common sulphide. "Czechoslovakia", Switzerland, Italy (large crystals up to 6 in/16 cm), Spain, UK, USA (New York, Pennsylvania, Illinois, Colorado and lesser amounts in many other states).

MOHS' HARDNESS: 6.0–6.5   **SPECIFIC GRAVITY:** 4.95–4.97   **CRYSTAL SYSTEM:** Cubic

A R S E N O P Y R I T E FeAsS to FeS₂.FeAs₂
SULPHIDE GROUP

DISTINCTIVE FEATURES Colour, streak. Also, when heated in an open tube, it gives off sulphurous fumes and produces a white sublimate of arsenic trioxide.
COLOUR Silvery tin white to iron grey.
LUSTRE Metallic.
STREAK Black to dark grey.
TRANSPARENCY Opaque.
CLEAVAGE Good on 110.
FRACTURE Uneven.
TENACITY Brittle.
FORMS Prismatic crystals, often flattened. Granular.
TWINNING On 110, occasionally on 101.
VARIETIES None.

USES Principal ore of arsenic.
OCCURRENCE Associated with cassiterite, wolframite, sphalerite and galena mineralized veins in granite and associated rocks. Also in limestones and dolomites and frequently associated with gold. Austria, Germany, Switzerland, Sweden, UK, Bolivia, Canada, USA (New Hampshire, Connecticut, Montana and Colorado).

MOHS' HARDNESS: 5.5–6.0   **SPECIFIC GRAVITY:** 5.9–6.2   **CRYSTAL SYSTEM:** Orthorhombic

PROUSTITE $3Ag_2S.As_2S_3$
SULPHIDE GROUP

DISTINCTIVE FEATURES Colour, streak and, when heated in a closed tube, it fuses, emits sulphurous fumes and leaves a white sublimate of arsenic trioxide.
COLOUR Dark red to vermilion.
LUSTRE Adamantine.
STREAK Same as colour.
TRANSPARENCY Transparent to translucent.
CLEAVAGE Good on $10\bar{1}1$.
FRACTURE Uneven to occasionally conchoidal.
TENACITY Brittle.
FORMS None.
TWINNING On $10\bar{1}4$ and 1011.
VARIETIES None.

USES Mineral collections.
OCCURRENCE In hydrothermal silver veins and associated with galena and sphalerite. "Czechoslovakia", Germany, France, Chile, Mexico, USA (though very rare).

MOHS' HARDNESS: 2.0–2.5

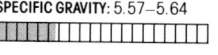

SPECIFIC GRAVITY: 5.57–5.64

CRYSTAL SYSTEM: Hexagonal

HALITE $NaCl$
HALIDE GROUP

DISTINCTIVE FEATURES Taste – it's the natural form of table salt – solubility, cleavage.
Note: Specimens will absorb atmospheric water and deliquesce if not kept in a sealed container.
COLOUR Colourless, white to yellowish-brown or shades of grey-blue.
LUSTRE Vitreous.
STREAK Same as colour.
TRANSPARENCY Transparent to translucent.
CLEAVAGE Perfect on 100.
FRACTURE Conchoidal.
TENACITY Brittle.
FORMS Cubes, often with sunken crystal faces. Massive, granular and compact.

TWINNING Interpenetrant.
VARIETIES None.
USES Principal source of common salt, but also in preparation of sodium compounds, glass and soap.
OCCURRENCE Worldwide as a main constituent of seawater. Commonly stratified up to 33 yds (30 m) in thickness in sedimentary rocks. Under pressure, the salt may flow upwards to produce huge salt domes at the surface. South East Russia, Poland, Austria, Germany, Switzerland, France, UK, Iran, India, Peru, Colombia, USA (New York, Wyoming, Michigan, Ohio, Lousiana, Kansas, Arizona, Nevada), Canada (Ontario).

MOHS' HARDNESS: 2.5

SPECIFIC GRAVITY: 2.1–2.6

CRYSTAL SYSTEM: Cubic

FLUORITE CaF₂
HALIDE GROUP

DISTINCTIVE FEATURES Excellent cubic form, cleavage and sometimes banded.

COLOUR Very variable: the pure form is colourless, but it also comes in all shades of blue, yellow, green and the colours are often banded.

LUSTRE Vitreous.

STREAK White.

TRANSPARENCY Transparent to subtransparent.

CLEAVAGE Perfect on 111.

FRACTURE Conchoidal to flat.

TENACITY Brittle.

FORMS Cubes and granular, massive and compact forms often show excellent colour banding.

TWINNING Interpenetrant on 111.

VARIETIES Blue John, which is a banded, blue, fibrous to columnar form, worked into ornaments and jewellery.

USES As flux in the steel industry, for enamelling, opal glass, manufacturing hydrofluoric acid and for ornaments and jewellery.

OCCURRENCE Mostly in minerallized veins associated with galena, sphalerite, calcite and quartz, especially in limestones. Also in granites as minute crystals. UK (only source of Blue John), Germany, Austria, Italy, France, Norway, USA (New Hampshire, Connecticut, Virginia, Kentucky, Missouri, Colorado), Canada (Ontario).

MOHS' HARDNESS: 4

SPECIFIC GRAVITY: 3.01–3.25

CRYSTAL SYSTEM:
Cubic

– VARIETIES –

Blue John

DOLOMITE CaMg(CO₃)₂ to CaCO₃.MgCO₃
CARBONATE GROUP

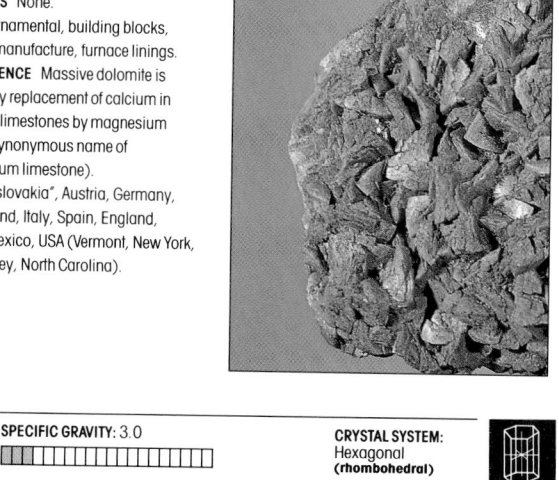

DISTINCTIVE FEATURES White to pale brownish saddle-shaped crystals that react to dilute, warm hydrochloric acid (care is needed when doing this).

COLOUR White when pure, otherwise brownish to reddish-brown or greenish to red, grey and black.

LUSTRE Vitreous to pearly.

STREAK Same as colour.

TRANSPARENCY Translucent (the transparent form is rare).

CLEAVAGE Perfect on 10Ī1.

FRACTURE Subconchoidal.

TENACITY Brittle.

FORMS Rhombohedrons or curved, saddle-like crystals. Granular to massive (often full of tiny cracks).

TWINNING On 0001 and 10Ī1.

VARIETIES None.

USES Ornamental, building blocks, cement manufacture, furnace linings.

OCCURRENCE Massive dolomite is formed by replacement of calcium in massive limestones by magnesium (hence synonymous name of magnesium limestone). "Czechoslovakia", Austria, Germany, Switzerland, Italy, Spain, England, Brazil, Mexico, USA (Vermont, New York, New Jersey, North Carolina).

MOHS' HARDNESS: 3.5–4.0

SPECIFIC GRAVITY: 3.0

CRYSTAL SYSTEM: Hexagonal **(rhombohedral)**

RHODOCHROSITE MnCO₃
CARBONATE GROUP

DISTINCTIVE FEATURES Rose-red coloured rhombohedral crystals in mineral veins, where it occurs as a secondary mineral.

COLOUR Pale rose-red to dark red, though yellowish-grey forms are known.

LUSTRE Vitreous to pearly.

STREAK White.

TRANSPARENCY Transparent to translucent.

CLEAVAGE Perfect on 10Ī1.

FRACTURE Uneven.

TENACITY Brittle.

FORMS Rhombohedral, but also massive, compact, granular and botryoidal.

TWINNING None.

VARIETIES None.

USES Mineral collections.

OCCURRENCE As a secondary mineral associated with lead and copper veins rich in manganese. Rather rare mineral. Romania, UK, Germany, USA (Connecticut, New Jersey, Michigan, Montana, Colorado).

MOHS' HARDNESS: 3.5–4.5

SPECIFIC GRAVITY: 3.5–3.6

CRYSTAL SYSTEM: Hexagonal

CALCITE CaCO₃
CARBONATE GROUP

DISTINCTIVE FEATURES Effervesces in dilute hydrochloric acid (take care doing this). Two excellent cleavages permit the mineral to break into perfect rhombohedrons and it fluoresces pale red under ultraviolet light, transparent forms being doubly refracting.

COLOUR Colourless to white. Also any combination of colours, due to impurities, even to black.

LUSTRE Vitreous to earthy.

STREAK white to grey.

TRANSPARENCY Transparent to opaque.

CLEAVAGE Perfect on $10\bar{1}\bar{1}$, giving rhombohedral-shaped fragments.

FRACTURE Difficult to obtain because of excellent cleavage.

TENACITY Brittle.

FORMS Nail-head spa, dog-tooth spa.

TWINNING On 0001, giving lamella twins.

VARIETIES Iceland Spa, which is transparent and doubly refracting. Calcite is the main component of limestone and varieties form in them — massive limestone, lithographic limestone, oolitic limestone, chalk, tufa, stalactites and stalagmites and marble.

USES Many, including cement manufacture, making building blocks, ornamental, furnace flux, polarizing Nicol prisms, whitewash, agriculture.

OCCURRENCE Worldwide in limestone rocks, but particularly in Austria, Germany, France, UK, Iceland, Ireland, Mexico, USA (New York, Ohio, Michigan, Illinois, Missouri, Dakota, Montana, Arizona).

– VARIETIES –

Iceland Spa showing double refraction

MOHS' HARDNESS: 3.0

SPECIFIC GRAVITY: 2.7

CRYSTAL SYSTEM: Hexagonal

CERUSSITE PbCO₃
CARBONATE GROUP

DISTINCTIVE FEATURES White, striated elongated prismatic crystals, often in small stellate groups. Reacts to nitric acid (take care doing this).
COLOUR Mostly white, but may be greenish or dark bluish-grey.
LUSTRE Adamantine.
STREAK No colour.
TRANSPARENCY Translucent to, rarely, transparent.
CLEAVAGE Good on 110 and 021.
FRACTURE Conchoidal (though this is difficult to see).
TENACITY Brittle.
FORMS Tabular to elongated prismatic crystals, often in stellar-shaped groups. Occasionally stalactitic.
TWINNING Common on 110 and 130.

VARIETIES None.
USES Lead ore.
OCCURRENCE In oxidized zones of lead-bearing veins, where lead ores have reacted with carbonate-rich water. Siberia, Austria, Germany, France, Scotland, Tunisia, Namibia, Australia, USA (Pennsylvania, Missouri, Colorado, Arizona, New Mexico).

MOHS' HARDNESS: 3.0–3.5

SPECIFIC GRAVITY: 6.5–6.6

CRYSTAL SYSTEM: Orthorhombic

MALACHITE CuCO₃.Cu(OH)₂
CARBONATE GROUP

DISTINCTIVE FEATURES Bright green, often botryoidal or stalactitic masses, associated with chalcopyrite and other copper ores such as azurite. Reacts to acids.
COLOUR Vivid, bright green (hence malachite green).
LUSTRE Crystals adamantine to vitreous, silky when fibrous, encrustations dull.
STREAK Bright green.
TRANSPARENCY Opaque to translucent.
CLEAVAGE Perfect on 001.
FRACTURE Subconchoidal to uneven.
TENACITY Brittle.
FORMS Rare crystals occur as acicular prismatic small tufts. Generally massive

or encrusting fibrous botryoidal masses. Sometimes stalactitic. Earthy encrustations on other copper ores.
TWINNING Common on 100.
VARIETIES None.
USES Copper ore, jewellery and small, carved ornaments.
OCCURRENCE Unoxidized zones of copper-bearing veins where other copper ores, such as chalcopyrite, have reacted with carbonate-rich water. The Urals in Russia, Romania, Germany, France, UK, Zaire, Zimbabwe, South Africa, Australia, USA (Pennsylvania, Tennessee, Arizona, Utah, Nevada).

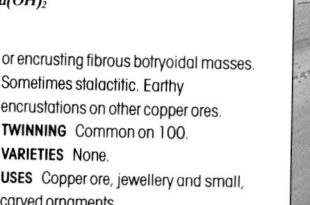

MOHS' HARDNESS: 3.5–4.0

SPECIFIC GRAVITY: 4.0

CRYSTAL SYSTEM: Monoclinic

A Z U R I T E $2CuCO_3.Cu(OH)_2$
CARBONATE GROUP

DISTINCTIVE FEATURES Vivid blue crystals in association with malachite and reacts to nitric acid (take care when doing this).

COLOUR Dark, vivid blue to cerulean blue.

LUSTRE Vitreous to adamantine.

STREAK Pale blue.

TRANSPARENCY Transparent to translucent.

CLEAVAGE Excellent on 021.

FRACTURE Conchoidal.

TENACITY Brittle.

FORMS Varied: slender prismatic crystals to granular, massive, columnar or earthy.

TWINNING Variable.

VARIETIES None.

USES As ore of copper and in mineral collections.

OCCURRENCE Associated with oxidized copper ores, invariably in association with malachite. Siberia, Greece, Romania, France, Scandinavia, Namibia, Australia, USA (Arizona, New Mexico).

MOHS' HARDNESS: 3.5–4.0

SPECIFIC GRAVITY: 3.8–3.9

CRYSTAL SYSTEM: Monoclinic

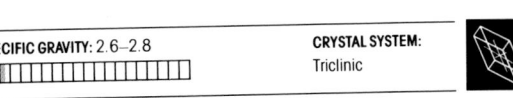

T U R Q U O I S E $CaAl_6(PO_4)_4(OH)_8.4H_2O$
PHOSPHATE GROUP

DISTINCTIVE FEATURES Cerulean blue to pale bluish-green nodular masses, or as seams in weathered lavas and pegmatites.

COLOUR Bright cerulean blue to pale, bluish-green.

LUSTRE Waxy.

STREAK White to pale green.

TRANSPARENCY Mostly opaque.

CLEAVAGE None.

FRACTURE Small-scale conchoidal.

TENACITY Brittle.

FORMS Botryoidal or reniform, stalactitic. Massive, small seams or fine grains.

TWINNING None.

VARIETIES None.

USES Jewellery, ornamental.

OCCURRENCE As small veins and masses in altered lavas or pegmatites and often associated with limonite and chalcedony. Iran, Siberia, France, Germany, USA (Arizona, California, Colorado, New Mexico, Virginia).

MOHS' HARDNESS: 5.0–6.0

SPECIFIC GRAVITY: 2.6–2.8

CRYSTAL SYSTEM: Triclinic

A P A T I T E $Ca_5(PO_4)_3(OH,F,Cl)$
PHOSPHATE GROUP

DISTINCTIVE FEATURES Usually found as pale green, six-sided prismatic crystals, often elongated, mostly in granitic pegmatites. Soluble in hydrochloric acid (take care when doing this).

COLOUR Mostly pale greenish-white, blue-green, brown or yellow.

LUSTRE Vitreous to resinous.

STREAK White.

TRANSPARENCY Transparent to opaque.

CLEAVAGE Poor on 0001.

FRACTURE Conchoidal to uneven.

TENACITY Brittle.

FORMS Usually short, prismatic six-sided crystals, but tabular, fibrous, granular and compact forms also occur.

TWINNING None.

VARIETIES Meroxite, which has blue to blue-green crystals, and francolite, which has tiny, curved crystals and stalactitic forms.

USES Source of phosphorus for agriculture and clear forms are used as gemstones.

OCCURRENCE Important accessory mineral of igneous rocks, but mostly metamorphosed limestones, acid igneous rocks and serpentines. Worldwide, particularly the Urals in Russia, "Czechoslovakia", Switzerland, Scandinavia, UK, Mexico, Iran, USA (Maine, Massachusetts, New York, California), Canada (Ontario, Quebec).

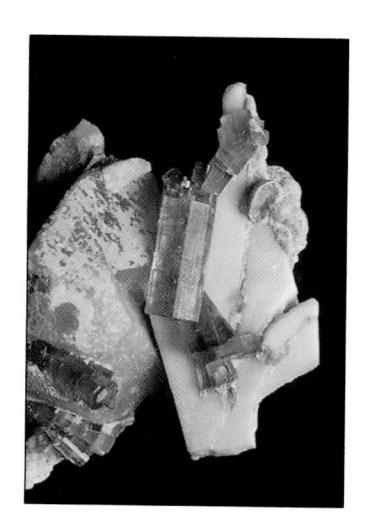

MOHS' HARDNESS: 5.0

SPECIFIC GRAVITY: 3.2–3.4

CRYSTAL SYSTEM: Hexagonal

P Y R O M O R P H I T E $Pb_5(PO_4,AsO_4)_3Cl$
PHOSPHATE GROUP

DISTINCTIVE FEATURES Small, yellowish-green, six-sided, prismatic crystals filling rock cavities in mineralized zones rich in lead.

COLOUR Pale yellowish-green usually, but also various shades of brown and yellow.

LUSTRE Resinous.

STREAK White to pale yellow.

TRANSPARENCY Subtransparent to translucent.

CLEAVAGE None.

FRACTURE Irregular.

TENACITY Brittle.

FORMS Six-sided prismatic or tabular crystals. Sometimes botryoidal, fibrous or granular.

TWINNING None.

VARIETIES According to form, eg fibrous pyromorphite.

USES Source of lead.

OCCURRENCE A sporadic secondary mineral in lead mineralized zones. Germany, France, Spain, UK, Australia, USA (Pennsylvania, North Carolina, Idaho).

MOHS' HARDNESS: 3.5–4.0

SPECIFIC GRAVITY: 7.0

CRYSTAL SYSTEM: Hexagonal

MIMETITE $3Pb_3As_2O_8.PbCl_2$
PHOSPHATE GROUP

DISTINCTIVE FEATURES Small, yellow to brownish-orange six-sided crystals with flat (0001) terminations found in areas where there are lead-rich metalliferous veins.

COLOUR Yellow to yellowish-brown to orange and, rarely, white.

LUSTRE Resinous.

STREAK White.

TRANSPARENCY Translucent, occasionally transparent.

CLEAVAGE Poor on $10\bar{1}1$.

FRACTURE Subconchoidal, but difficult to see because of small size of the crystals.

TENACITY Brittle.

FORMS Usually six-sided prismatic crystals, but sometimes as mammillated or globular forms encrusting rocks.

TWINNING None.

VARIETIES Campylite, which has yellowish-brown-red crystals – found only in UK.

USES Source of lead.

OCCURRENCE Associated with lead carbonates and limonite in areas of lead-rich veins. Austria, Siberia, "Czechoslovakia", Germany, UK, France, Africa, Mexico, USA (Pennsylvania, Utah).

MOHS' HARDNESS: 3.5

SPECIFIC GRAVITY: 7.0

CRYSTAL SYSTEM: Hexagonal

VANADINITE $Pb_5(VO_4)_3Cl$
PHOSPHATE GROUP

DISTINCTIVE FEATURES Six-sided prismatic red to straw-coloured crystals associated with areas of secondary lead deposits.

COLOUR Various shades of red to yellowish-brown.

LUSTRE Resinous to adamantine.

STREAK White to yellow.

TRANSPARENCY Subtransparent (darker colours are opaque).

CLEAVAGE None.

FRACTURE Uneven.

TENACITY Brittle.

FORMS Six-sided prismatic crystals. The 0001th face is often hollow. Also found as rock encrustations.

TWINNING None.

VARIETIES None.

USES Source of vanadium and lead.

OCCURRENCE Rather rare mineral, found in areas of secondary lead deposits. Mexico, Argentina, the Urals in Russia, Austria, UK, Zaire, USA (Arizona, New Mexico, South Dakota).

MOHS' HARDNESS: 2.7–3.0

SPECIFIC GRAVITY: 6.5–7.0

CRYSTAL SYSTEM: Hexagonal

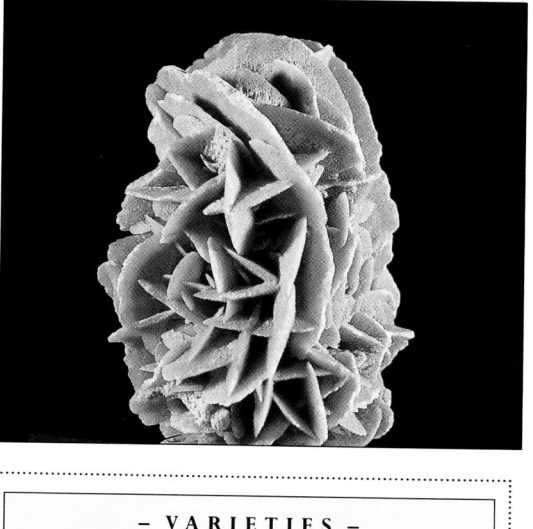

GYPSUM CaSO₄.2H₂O

SULPHATE GROUP

DISTINCTIVE FEATURES Soft enough to be scratched by a finger nail. When it is heated in an open tube, it gives off water. There is no reaction to acid.

COLOUR White to pale grey and shades of pinkish-red.

LUSTRE Pearly to glistening or dull and earthy.

STREAK White.

TRANSPARENCY Transparent to opaque.

CLEAVAGE Excellent on 010.

FRACTURE Conchoidal, sometimes fibrous.

TENACITY Crumbly.

FORMS Massive, flat or elongated, generally prismatic, crystals. Swallow-tailed twins are common and distinctive.

TWINNING Good on 100, giving swallow-tailed twins.

VARIETIES Selenite, which has transparent, distinct, bladed crystals, satin spa, which has pearly, fibrous masses, and alabaster, which is fine-grained and slightly coloured.

USES Medical (source of plaster of Paris), for manufacturing wall plaster used in building trade, ornamental carvings made from alabaster.

OCCURRENCE As beds, sometimes massive, in sedimentary rocks, such as limestones, shales and clays. UK, France, Russia, USA (New York, Kentucky, Michigan, Kansas, Dakota and Utah).

- VARIETIES -

Satin Spa

Selenite

MOHS' HARDNESS: 1.5–2.0

SPECIFIC GRAVITY: 2.3

CRYSTAL SYSTEM:
Monoclinic

BARYTES BaSO₄
SULPHATE GROUP

DISTINCTIVE FEATURES High density, pale greenish-white to pale brownish tabular crystals. Also appears as desert roses of radiating pale brown crystals. Hardness.

COLOUR White to greenish-white or pale brownish-red.

LUSTRE Vitreous to resinous.

STREAK White.

TRANSPARENCY Transparent to opaque.

CLEAVAGE Perfect on 001 and 110.

FRACTURE Uneven.

TENACITY Brittle.

FORMS Often occurs as groups of tabular or bladed crystals. Also massive, encrusting, banded, mammillary and fibrous.

TWINNING None.

VARIETIES None.

USES Barium ore, for refining sugar, for drilling mud in the oil industry, for medical barium meals for x-ray, as pigment, in the paper industry.

OCCURRENCE In veins and beds associated with ores of lead, copper, zinc and iron. Common gangue mineral in metalliferous veins. It is associated with fluorite, quartz, calcite, dolomite and stibnite. "Czechoslovakia", Romania, France, Spain, England, USA (Connecticut, New York, Pennsylvania, Michigan and Dakota).

MOHS' HARDNESS: 3.0–3.5

SPECIFIC GRAVITY: 4.4–4.6

CRYSTAL SYSTEM: Orthorhombic

CROCOITE PbCrO₄
CHROMATE GROUP

DISTINCTIVE FEATURES Pinkish-red elongated prismatic crystals, often in masses.

COLOUR Shades of pinkish-red to bright saffron-coppery pink.

LUSTRE Adamantine to vitreous.

STREAK Yellowish-orange.

TRANSPARENCY Transparent.

CLEAVAGE Good on 110.

FRACTURE Uneven, sometimes conchoidal.

TENACITY Sectile.

FORMS Elongated, prismatic crystals. Also columnar or granular.

TWINNING None.

VARIETIES None.

USES Mineral collections.

OCCURRENCE Secondary minerals deposited by mineralizing waters that have leached lead from adjacent veins. The Urals in Russia, Romania, Tasmania, Philippines, USA (Arizona, California).

MOHS' HARDNESS: 2.5–3.0

SPECIFIC GRAVITY: 5.9–6.1

CRYSTAL SYSTEM: Monoclinic

WOLFRAMITE (Fe,Mn)WO₄
TUNGSTATE GROUP

DISTINCTIVE FEATURES Well-formed, tabular or prismatic, silvery black crystals in metalliferous sulphide and pegmatite veins in granites.
COLOUR Black to very dark grey.
LUSTRE Submetallic.
STREAK Black.
TRANSPARENCY Opaque.
CLEAVAGE Good on 010.
FRACTURE Uneven to rough.
TENACITY Brittle.
FORMS Mostly as tabular crystals, but prismatic forms also occur.
TWINNING None.
VARIETIES None.
USES Source of tungsten.
OCCURRENCE In metalliferous veins, cavities and pegmatites in granites, where it is associated with cassiterite and copper ores. Worldwide, China, UK, Malaya, Australia, Portugal, Burma, Bolivia, USA (Colorado, New Mexico, Nevada, Connecticut).

MOHS' HARDNESS: 4.0–4.5	SPECIFIC GRAVITY: 7.0	CRYSTAL SYSTEM: Monoclinic

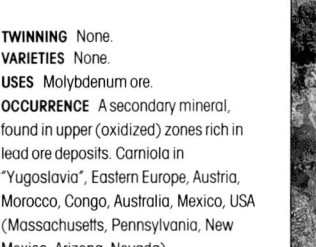

WULFENITE Pb(MoO₄,WO₄)
TUNGSTATE GROUP

DISTINCTIVE FEATURES Usually as thin, tabular brownish-yellow to orange crystals, associated with lead ore deposits.
COLOUR Bright orange to brownish-yellow to brown.
LUSTRE Resinous to adamantine.
STREAK White.
TRANSPARENCY Subtransparent to translucent.
CLEAVAGE Good on 111.
FRACTURE Subconchoidal, but difficult to see with the naked eye.
TENACITY Brittle.
FORMS Usually thin, square, tabular to octahedral or prismatic crystals, but granular and compact forms also occur.
TWINNING None.
VARIETIES None.
USES Molybdenum ore.
OCCURRENCE A secondary mineral, found in upper (oxidized) zones rich in lead ore deposits. Carniola in "Yugoslavia", Eastern Europe, Austria, Morocco, Congo, Australia, Mexico, USA (Massachusetts, Pennsylvania, New Mexico, Arizona, Nevada).

MOHS' HARDNESS: 2.5–3.0	SPECIFIC GRAVITY: 6.5–8.0	CRYSTAL SYSTEM: Tetragonal

ZIRCON ZrSiO₄
SILICATE GROUP

DISTINCTIVE FEATURES Usually pale to deep brown short prisms with pyramidal terminations. Mostly small crystals with adamantine lustre.
COLOUR Various shades of brown, to blue, green or colourless.
LUSTRE Adamantine.
STREAK No colour.
TRANSPARENCY Transparent to opaque.
CLEAVAGE Poor on 110.
FRACTURE Conchoidal. Often difficult to see because of small crystal size.
TENACITY Brittle.
FORMS Short prisms with pyramidal terminations.
TWINNING As geniculate twins.
VARIETIES Hyacinth, which is red to orange.

USES Gemstone, with colourless forms being used as imitation diamonds.
OCCURRENCE Important accessory mineral in acid igneous rocks. Because of its hardness and resistance to weathering, it also occurs in sandstones, especially those bearing gold. Worldwide, mostly associated with coarsely crystalline granitic rocks.

MOHS' HARDNESS: 7.5

SPECIFIC GRAVITY: 4.5–5.0

CRYSTAL SYSTEM: Tetragonal

EPIDOTE Ca₂Fe(Al₂O)(OH)(Si₂O₇)(SiO₄)
SILICATE GROUP

DISTINCTIVE FEATURES Deep green to black, elongated and striated, prismatic crystals occurring in fibrous or granular masses in contact-metamorphosed limestones.
COLOUR Emerald green to pistachio green to reddish or yellow.
LUSTRE Vitreous to resinous.
STREAK None.
TRANSPARENCY Subtransparent to opaque (transparent varieties rare).
CLEAVAGE Perfect on 001.
FRACTURE Uneven.
TENACITY Brittle.
FORMS Elongated and striated clusters of prismatic crystals. Also massive.
TWINNING Common on 100.

VARIETIES Crystals, fibrous, massive. Withamite, which is bright red to pale yellow, and chrome epidote, which is emerald green to lemon yellow.
USES Mineral collections.
OCCURRENCE In contact-metamorphic zones, in regionally metamorphosed rocks, such as gneisses and schists. Worldwide, but particularly the Urals in Russia, France, Norway, USA (Connecticut, Colorado, California, Alaska).

MOHS' HARDNESS: 6.0–7.0

SPECIFIC GRAVITY: 3.3–3.5

CRYSTAL SYSTEM: Monoclinic

GARNET $XAl_2Si_3O_{12}$ (where $X=Ca_3,Mg_3,Fe_3,Mn_3,Fe_2,Cr_2$)
SILICATE GROUP

DISTINCTIVE FEATURES Crystal shape, colour, rock association.

COLOUR Deep red to pale yellowish-red, black, deep or bright green.

LUSTRE Resinous to glassy.

STREAK White.

TRANSPARENCY Transparent to translucent to opaque.

CLEAVAGE None.

FRACTURE Uneven and occasionally subconchoidal.

TENACITY Brittle.

FORMS Dodecahedron and trapezohedrons.

TWINNING None.

VARIETIES Grossularite, which is pale green to amber to deep brown, pyrope, which is blood red to black, almandine, which is brownish-red to black, spessartite, which is dark red to brownish-red, andradite, which is shades of red, yellow, green, brown and black, and uvarovite, which is emerald green (rare).

USES Gemstone.

OCCURRENCE Widespread in many rocks. Some of the best crystals are from schist, serpentines, metamorphosed limestones, gneisses and granite pegmatites. Worldwide, but grossularite is very common in schists and metamorphosed limestones, pyrope in South Africa, almandine in USA (New York), spessartite in Germany and Italy, andradite in Sweden, Germany, the Urals and USA (New Jersey), uvarovite in the Urals in Russia, Canada (Quebec), Spain, Scandinavia, West Africa.

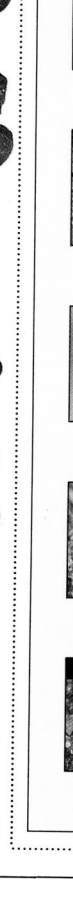

Pyrope

– VARIETIES –

Grossularite

Almandine

Spessartite

Uvarovite

Andradite

MOHS' HARDNESS: 6.5–7.2

SPECIFIC GRAVITY: 3.0–4.0

CRYSTAL SYSTEM: Cubic

OLIVINE X₂SiO₄ (where X=Mg or Fe)
SILICATE GROUP

DISTINCTIVE FEATURES Colour, rock association.
COLOUR Green to olive green, yellow – brownish-red when oxidized.
LUSTRE Vitreous.
STREAK Usually white, sometimes pale yellow – red when oxidized.
TRANSPARENCY Transparent to translucent.
CLEAVAGE Normally on 010, but occasionally on 100.
FRACTURE Conchoidal.
TENACITY Brittle.
FORMS Crystals rarely elongated parallel to C axis, often flat. Also granular or massive, especially in peridotite.
TWINNING Rare.

VARIETIES Forsterite, which is white, green or yellow, and fayalite, which is greenish-yellow to black.
USES As a gemstone (peridot) when transparent green.
OCCURRENCE In basic igneous rocks low in silica and magnesium. Italy, Germany, Austria, Norway, Egypt, Red Sea, Burma, Brazil, USA (Vermont, North Carolina, Arizona, New Mexico). Common in volcanic rocks worldwide.

MOHS' HARDNESS: 6.5–7

SPECIFIC GRAVITY: 3.27–3.37

CRYSTAL SYSTEM: Orthorhombic

DIOPTASE CuSiO₂(OH)₂
SILICATE GROUP

DISTINCTIVE FEATURES Deep emerald green, short prismatic crystals and found in association with deposits of copper sulphides. A somewhat rare mineral.
COLOUR Deep to medium emerald green.
LUSTRE Vitreous.
STREAK Green.
TRANSPARENCY Transparent to translucent.
CLEAVAGE Perfect on 10$\bar{1}$1.
FRACTURE Conchoidal, but difficult to see as the crystals are either too small or too valuable to break.
TENACITY Brittle.
FORMS Short, prismatic, six-sided crystals. Also massive or in granular clusters.

TWINNING None.
VARIETIES None.
USES Much-prized by mineral collectors.
OCCURRENCE In upper, oxidized zones of copper ore deposits, where excellent (but rare) crystals occur in drusy cavities. Russia, the Congo, Chile, USA (Arizona).

MOHS' HARDNESS: 5.0

SPECIFIC GRAVITY: 3.3

CRYSTAL SYSTEM: Hexagonal

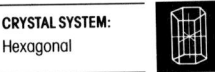

KYANITE Al_2OSiO_4
SILICATE GROUP

DISTINCTIVE FEATURES Translucent, pale blue, lath-shaped crystals. Hardness along length is less than across crystal. Often associated with staurolite in schists.

COLOUR Pale cerulean blue, sometimes with white margins.

LUSTRE Vitreous to pearly.

STREAK None.

TRANSPARENCY Translucent to transparent.

CLEAVAGE Perfect on 100.

FRACTURE Not applicable.

TENACITY Brittle.

FORMS Long, bladed or lath-shaped crystals.

TWINNING None.

VARIETIES None.

USES In refractory materials for furnaces, because of its high melting point, and jewellery.

OCCURRENCE In mica schists resulting from regional metamorphism, often in association with staurolite, garnet and corundum. The Urals in Russia, European Alps, USA (Carolina).

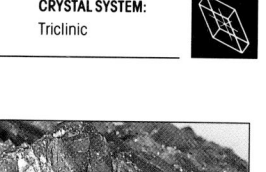

MOHS' HARDNESS: 4 (along length parallel to C axis); 7 (across width parallel to B axis)	SPECIFIC GRAVITY: 4	CRYSTAL SYSTEM: Triclinic

STAUROLITE $(Fe,Mg)_2(AlFe)_9O_6.(SiO_4(O,OH)_2$
SILICATE GROUP

DISTINCTIVE FEATURES Mostly opaque to deep red stumpy prisms or cruciform twins in mica schists resulting from regional metamorphism. Often associated with kyanite, garnet and quartz. Crystal surfaces often rough.

COLOUR Deep wine red to brown or yellow.

LUSTRE Resinous to poorly vitreous.

STREAK No colour.

TRANSPARENCY Mostly opaque, but sometimes translucent.

CLEAVAGE Good on 010.

FRACTURE Subconchoidal, but this is difficult to see because the crystals are small.

TENACITY Brittle.

FORMS Stumpy or flattened prismatic crystals and cruciform twins.

TWINNING Cruciform twins on 032.

VARIETIES None.

USES Rarely as a gemstone.

OCCURRENCE In schists of regionally metamorphosed zones. Associated with kyanite, garnet, quartz and tourmaline. Worldwide, but particularly in Switzerland, France, USA (New England, New Hampshire, Massachusetts, Virginia, Carolina).

MOHS' HARDNESS: 7.0–7.5	SPECIFIC GRAVITY: 3.6–3.8	CRYSTAL SYSTEM: Orthorhombic

ANDALUSITE Al_2OSiO_4
SILICATE GROUP

DISTINCTIVE FEATURES Elongated glassy prisms in slates, hornfels and schists of contact metamorphism zones associated with granite intrusions. Also found in gneisses and schists in regionally metamorphosed zones.

COLOUR Clear to white, but also pale red, brown and green.

LUSTRE Vitreous.

STREAK No colour.

TRANSPARENCY Transparent to opaque.

CLEAVAGE Perfect on 110, poor on 100.

FRACTURE Uneven.

TENACITY Brittle.

FORMS As elongated prisms – square forms not so common.

TWINNING None.

VARIETIES Chiastolite, which has fat, elongated crystals with an internal pale or coloured cross running along the length of each one.

USES Gemstone when clear.

OCCURRENCE In zones of contact metamorphism surrounding granite masses. Also in gneisses and schists resulting from regional metamorphism. Worldwide, but particularly the Urals in Russia, European Alps, France (Pyrenées), Australia, Brazil, USA (Maine, Massachusetts, Pennsylvania, California).

MOHS' HARDNESS: 7.5

SPECIFIC GRAVITY: 3.1

CRYSTAL SYSTEM: Orthorhombic

TOPAZ $Al_2(SiO_4)(OH,F)_2$
SILICATE GROUP

DISTINCTIVE FEATURES Pale amber to clear prismatic crystals with a perfect basal cleavage on 001. Occurs in granite pegmatites together with tourmaline, beryl and fluorite.

COLOUR Pale honey-yellow to pale orange-yellow, clear with hint of blue or colourless. A pale green and pink form is known.

LUSTRE Vitreous.

STREAK No colour.

TRANSPARENCY Transparent to subtransparent.

CLEAVAGE Perfect on 001 (known as basal cleavage).

FRACTURE Subconchoidal to uneven.

TENACITY Brittle.

FORMS Stumpy prismatic crystals, often with striated faces along their length.

TWINNING None.

VARIETIES None.

USES Gemstone.

OCCURRENCE Acid igneous rocks, such as granite, where crystals may occur in pegmatite or druses. Often associated with fluorite, cassiterite and beryl. The Urals in Russia, Germany, Nigeria, Australia, Japan, USA (Maine, New Hampshire, Connecticut, Texas, Virginia, Utah, California).

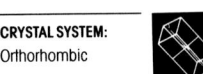

MOHS' HARDNESS: 8.0

SPECIFIC GRAVITY: 3.5–3.6

CRYSTAL SYSTEM: Orthorhombic

TOURMALINE $Na(Mg,Fe,Mn,Li,Al)_3Al(Si_6O_{18})(BO_3)_3.(OH,F)_4$

SILICATE GROUP

DISTINCTIVE FEATURES Elongated, well-striated, prismatic crystals in granites and pegmatites. Colour varies from black to green and pink.

COLOUR Mostly black, but also dark brown, violet, green and pink and some forms are bicoloured pinkish-red and green.

LUSTRE Vitreous, sometimes resinous.

STREAK No colour.

TRANSPARENCY Transparent to opaque.

CLEAVAGE All very poor.

FRACTURE Poor conchoidal, uneven.

TENACITY Brittle.

FORMS Parallel elongated or acicular prisms, sometimes radiating. Also massive (mostly schorl) and as scattered grains in granites.

TWINNING None.

VARIETIES Schorl, which is black, rubellite, which is pink, indicolite, which is deep violet-blue, Brazilian emerald, which is emerald green, and dravite, which is brown.

USES As gemstones when perfectly transparent.

OCCURRENCE In pegmatites and drusy cavities in granites and gneisses, where it has crystallized from late-stage mineralizing fluids and gases. The Urals in Siberia, Germany, Greenland, "Czechoslovakia", Switzerland, UK, Ceylon, Brazil, USA (New England, California).

Schorl

MOHS' HARDNESS: 7.0	SPECIFIC GRAVITY: 3.2	CRYSTAL SYSTEM: Hexagonal

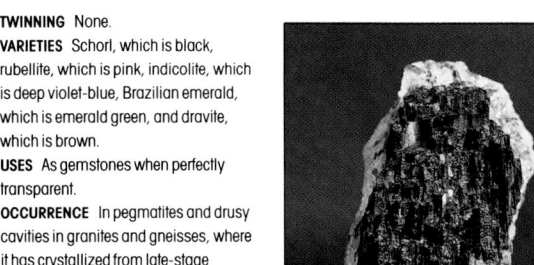

– VARIETIES –

Dravite

Rubellite

Green Tourmaline

Indicolite

EMERALD $Be_3Al_2Si_4O_{18}$
SILICATE GROUP

DISTINCTIVE FEATURES Emerald green, often six-sided barrel-shaped prismatic crystals. Occurs in pegmatites or drusy cavities in granitic rocks.
COLOUR Emerald green.
LUSTRE Vitreous.
STREAK White.
TRANSPARENCY Transparent to subtranslucent.
CLEAVAGE Poor on 0001.
FRACTURE Poor conchoidal to uneven.
TENACITY Brittle.
FORMS Six-sided prismatic crystals, often barrel-shaped, sometimes granular.
TWINNING None.
VARIETIES None.

USES Gemstone.
OCCURRENCE In pegmatites and drusy cavities in granites. Sometimes found associated with topaz in mica schists. Russia, Austria, Germany, South Africa, Zambia, Zimbabwe, Colombia (the only locality where emeralds occur in limestone), USA (North Carolina – imperfect forms).

MOHS' HARDNESS: 7.0–7.5
SPECIFIC GRAVITY: 2.5–2.8
CRYSTAL SYSTEM: Hexagonal

AQUAMARINE $Be_3Al_2Si_6O_{18}$
SILICATE GROUP

DISTINCTIVE FEATURES Delicate bluish-green (aquamarine) hexagonal prisms in granite pegmatites and drusy cavities.
COLOUR Pale blue-green (aquamarine).
LUSTRE Vitreous to resinous.
STREAK White.

TRANSPARENCY Transparent to translucent.
CLEAVAGE Poor on 0001.
FRACTURE Uneven to subconchoidal.
TENACITY Brittle.
FORMS Elongated hexagonal prisms. Also granular and compact forms.
TWINNING None.
VARIETIES None.
USES Gemstone.
OCCURRENCE In pegmatites and drusy cavities in granites. The Urals in Minsk, Madagascar, Brazil, Pakistan, USA (Massachusetts, Colorado).

MOHS' HARDNESS: 7.5–8.0
SPECIFIC GRAVITY: 2.7
CRYSTAL SYSTEM: Hexagonal

C O R D I E R I T E $Mg_2Al_4Si_5O_{18}$
SILICATE GROUP

DISTINCTIVE FEATURES Hardness, pseudohexagonal barrel-shaped crystals and vitreous lustre. Usually found as pseudomorphs of pinite (indefinite clay minerals) and mica.

COLOUR Pale greyish-blue to dark greyish-blue.

LUSTRE Vitreous.

STREAK None.

TRANSPARENCY Translucent to transparent.

CLEAVAGE Good on 010.

FRACTURE Subconchoidal, often difficult to see clearly.

TENACITY Brittle.

FORMS Stumpy pseudohexagonal barrel-shaped crystals. Also massive.

TWINNING On 110 and 130.

VARIETIES Also known as iolite and dichroite.

USES Gemstone, when transparent.

OCCURRENCE Mostly in acid igneous rocks, including schists and gneisses. Scandinavia, Austria, Greenland, Ceylon, USA (Connecticut).

MOHS' HARDNESS: 7–8

SPECIFIC GRAVITY: 2.57–2.68

CRYSTAL SYSTEM: Orthorhombic

A U G I T E $(Ca,Mg,Fe,Ti,Al)_2(Si,Al)_2O_6$
SILICATE GROUP

DISTINCTIVE FEATURES Dark colour, cyrstalline shape, rock association, 90 degree cleavage.

COLOUR Green to brownish-black.

LUSTRE Vitreous to resinous.

STREAK White to grey to greenish.

TRANSPARENCY Transparent to opaque.

CLEAVAGE Perfect on 110 at 90 degrees, often seen only in basal thin sections.

FRACTURE Conchoidal to uneven.

TENACITY Not applicable.

FORMS Fat, prismatic crystals, sometimes tabular on 100.

TWINNING Contact twins on 100 common.

VARIETIES Aegirine-augite, which is green to yellow, and fassaite, which is deep green.

USES As important rock-forming mineral in nature.

OCCURRENCE Worldwide in most basic igneous rocks, but ankaramite often yields large specimens up to 3 in (8 cm).

MOHS' HARDNESS: 5–6

SPECIFIC GRAVITY: 3.2–3.6

CRYSTAL SYSTEM: Monoclinic

RHODONITE $MnSiO_3$
SILICATE GROUP

DISTINCTIVE FEATURES Distinctive pink tabular crystals, often associated with rhodochrosite or tetrahedrite in metamorphic rocks.
COLOUR Rose-pink to red and, rarely, green-yellow.
LUSTRE Vitreous.
STREAK White.

TRANSPARENCY Usually translucent, though transparent forms do occur.
CLEAVAGE Perfect on 110.
FRACTURE Uneven to conchoidal.
TENACITY Brittle.
FORMS Usually as clusters of large tabular crystals.
TWINNING On 001.

VARIETIES None.
USES Ornamental.
OCCURRENCE In manganese ores associated with rhodochrosite or tetrahedrite. The Urals in Russia, Romania, Sweden, Australia, Mexico, USA (Massachusetts, New Jersey).

MOHS' HARDNESS: 5.5–6.5

SPECIFIC GRAVITY: 3.6

CRYSTAL SYSTEM: Triclinic

SPODUMENE $LiAl(SiO_3)_2$
SILICATE GROUP

DISTINCTIVE FEATURES In lithium-rich granite pegmatites as prismatic white, greenish-white or pale purple fat prismatic and often large crystals.
COLOUR White, often with central areas of pale lilac or green.
LUSTRE Vitreous.
STREAK White.
TRANSPARENCY Transparent to subtransparent.
CLEAVAGE Perfect on 110.
FRACTURE Uneven.
TENACITY Brittle.
FORMS Prismatic, often flattened on 100.
TWINNING None.
VARIETIES Hiddenite, which is pale yellow to emerald green, and kunzite, which is pale to deep lilac.
USES Gemstone.
OCCURRENCE In lithium-rich granite pegmatites. Scandinavia, Iceland, Brazil, Madagascar, USA (Maine, Massachusetts, Connecticut, North Carolina).

MOHS' HARDNESS: 6.5–7.0

SPECIFIC GRAVITY: 3.2

CRYSTAL SYSTEM: Monoclinic

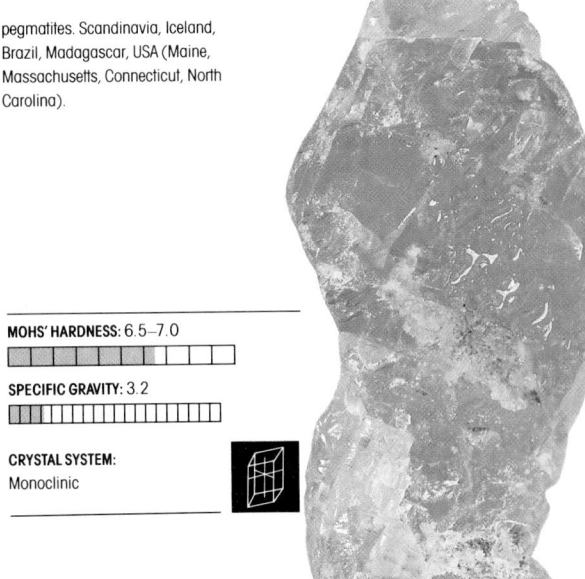

HORNBLENDE (Ca,Na,K)$_{2-3}$(Mg,Fe,Al)$_5$(Si,Al)$_8$O$_{22}$(OH,F)$_2$
SILICATE GROUP

DISTINCTIVE FEATURES Common mineral in igneous rocks, where it occurs as black to dark green stubby, prismatic crystals, although elongated forms are not uncommon. Distinguished in basal section from augite by its two cleavages that intersect at 120 degrees.

COLOUR Black to green-black and dark brown.

LUSTRE Vitreous, but often dull.

STREAK No colour.

TRANSPARENCY Opaque. Occasionally subtransparent.

CLEAVAGE Perfect on 110 directions. Intersect at 120 degrees.

FRACTURE Subconchoidal.

TENACITY Brittle.

FORMS Stubby, prismatic crystals.

Fibrous, granular and massive.

TWINNING Common on 100.

VARIETIES Hornblende is the most common member of the amphibole group of minerals. Other forms in the group include common hornblende, which is black, basaltic hornblende, which is deep green, riebeckite, which is dark blue-black, and asbestos, which is a fibrous-flaxy form in various colours.

USES Mineral collections.

OCCURRENCE An important component of many igneous rocks. Indeed, the classification of these rocks is based on the presence or absence of hornblende. Worldwide in igneous and metamorphic rocks.

MOHS' HARDNESS: 5.0–6.0

SPECIFIC GRAVITY: 3.0–3.5

CRYSTAL SYSTEM: Monoclinic

CROCIDOLITE Na(Al,Fe)(SiO$_3$)$_2$ with (Mg,Fe)SiO$_3$
SILICATE GROUP

DISTINCTIVE FEATURES Glistening fibrous to hair-like blue to green crystals.

COLOUR Medium to pale blue to medium green.

LUSTRE Silky.

STREAK Bluish.

TRANSPARENCY Transparent.

CLEAVAGE Perfect on 110.

FRACTURE Uneven.

TENACITY Brittle to flexible.

FORMS Fibrous masses of thin, prismatic crystals.

TWINNING None.

VARIETIES Synonymous is blue asbestos and when it is replaced by quartz it forms the mineral tiger's eye.

USES Mineral collections.

OCCURRENCE In veins and pegmatites in granites and syenites. South Africa, Austria, France, Bolivia, UK, USA (Massachusetts).

MOHS' HARDNESS: 6.0

SPECIFIC GRAVITY: 3.0

CRYSTAL SYSTEM: Monoclinic

47

MUSCOVITE $KAl_2(Si_3Al)O_{10}(OH)_2$
SILICATE GROUP

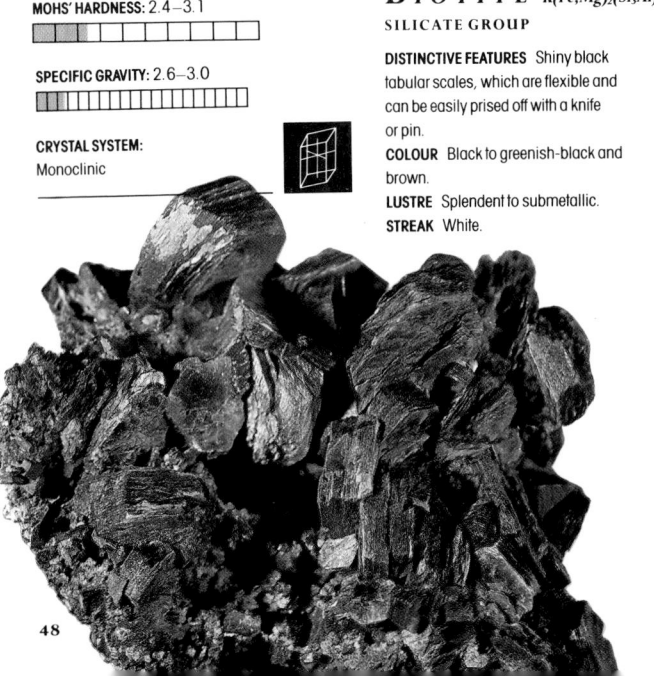

DISTINCTIVE FEATURES Shiny, silvery, platy mineral. The plates are flexible and can easily be prised off with a knife blade or pin. Common in granites and related rocks.

COLOUR Colourless to pale brown or green or yellow. Pale red varieties are also known.

LUSTRE Vitreous to pearly.

STREAK No colour.

TRANSPARENCY Transparent to translucent.

CLEAVAGE Perfect on 010.

FRACTURE Tends to bend without breaking.

TENACITY Flexible, elastic.

FORMS Usually tabular; may occur as tapering book of tabular crystals.

TWINNING On 001 (easily cleavable).

VARIETIES None.

USES Electrical insulators, furnace and stove windows.

OCCURRENCE An important component of many igneous and metamorphic rocks, especially acid igneous rocks, schists and gneisses. Occurs in granite pegmatites as large book-like masses. Worldwide.

MOHS' HARDNESS: 2.5–3.0

SPECIFIC GRAVITY: 2.7–3.0

CRYSTAL SYSTEM: Monoclinic

MOHS' HARDNESS: 2.4–3.1

SPECIFIC GRAVITY: 2.6–3.0

CRYSTAL SYSTEM: Monoclinic

BIOTITE $K(Fe,Mg)_2(Si_3Al)O_{10}(OH)_2$
SILICATE GROUP

DISTINCTIVE FEATURES Shiny black tabular scales, which are flexible and can be easily prised off with a knife or pin.

COLOUR Black to greenish-black and brown.

LUSTRE Splendent to submetallic.

STREAK White.

TRANSPARENCY Transparent to opaque.

CLEAVAGE Perfect on 001.

FRACTURE Tends to bend before breaking.

TENACITY Flexible, elastic.

FORMS Usually tabular.

TWINNING On 001, along which it is also easily cleaved.

VARIETIES None.

USES Mineral collections.

OCCURRENCE Important component of most igneous rocks, from granite to gabbro and their fine-grained equivalents. Found in granite pegmatites as large book-like masses. Worldwide.

PHLOGOPITE K(Mg,Fe)₃(Si₃Al)O₁₀(OH)₂
SILICATE GROUP

DISTINCTIVE FEATURES Shiny, coppery-brown, patchy black, platy mineral. The plates are flexible and easily prised off with a knife point or pin. Flakes often show a starlike figure in transmitted light.

COLOUR Coppery-brown to yellowish-brown, with much darker patches.

LUSTRE Pearly and sometimes slightly metallic.

STREAK No colour.

TRANSPARENCY Transparent to subtransparent.

CLEAVAGE Perfect on 001.

FRACTURE Bends without breaking.

TENACITY Flexible, elastic.

FORMS Tabular, scaly masses. Often seen as small flakes in acid igneous rocks.

TWINNING On 001, along which it is easily cleaved.

VARIETIES None.

USES Mineral collections.

OCCURRENCE A product of metamorphism. Occurs in serpentine, granular limestones and dolomites. Romania, Switzerland, Italy, Scandinavia, Finland, Ceylon, Madagascar, USA (New York, New Jersey), Canada (Ontario, Quebec).

MOHS' HARDNESS: 3.0

SPECIFIC GRAVITY: 2.8–3.0

CRYSTAL SYSTEM: Monoclinic

PREHNITE Ca₂Al(AlSi₃)O₁₀(OH)₂
SILICATE GROUP

DISTINCTIVE FEATURES Pale green botryoidal or reniform masses of small tabular crystals. Often stalactitic or in radiating clusters.

COLOUR Pale green to whitish-grey, the colour fading on exposure to air.

LUSTRE Vitreous.

STREAK No colour.

TRANSPARENCY Usually translucent, rarely subtransparent.

CLEAVAGE Not applicable.

FRACTURE Uneven to rough.

TENACITY Brittle.

FORMS Tabular, often barrel-shaped crystals; often globular or in radiating clusters.

TWINNING None.

VARIETIES None.

USES Mineral collections.

OCCURRENCE Mostly as a secondary mineral in basic igneous rocks and gneisses. Austria, Italy, Germany, France, UK, South Africa, USA (Massachusetts, Connecticut, New Jersey, Michigan).

MOHS' HARDNESS: 6.0–6.5

SPECIFIC GRAVITY: 2.9

CRYSTAL SYSTEM: Orthorhombic

QUARTZ *SiO₂*

SILICATE GROUP

DISTINCTIVE FEATURES Shape, rock association, hardness.

COLOUR Colourless when pure, but otherwise white, yellow, red, brown, green, blue, black.

LUSTRE Vitreous.

STREAK White or same as colour when coloured.

TRANSPARENCY Transparent to opaque.

CLEAVAGE Not seen.

FRACTURE Conchoidal.

TENACITY Brittle.

FORMS Prismatic and terminated by rhombohedrons that look like hexagonal pyramids.

TWINNING On C axis with crystals parallel.

VARIETIES Rock crystal, which is clear, glass-like, amethyst, which is purple, rose quartz, which is rose, citrine, which is yellow, smoky, which is dark brown, chalcedony, which is wax-like, plasma, which is green, agate, which is banded colours, flint, which is opaque black-brown and jasper, which is various colours.

USES Manufacture of glass and porcelain, ornamental, jewellery, abrasives, sand in mortar, sandstone in building.

OCCURRENCE Universal, mainly as sand. Smoky quartz is mainly found in the Swiss Alps, amethyst in the Alps, Brazil, USA (Maine, Virginia, Arkansas).

– VARIETIES –

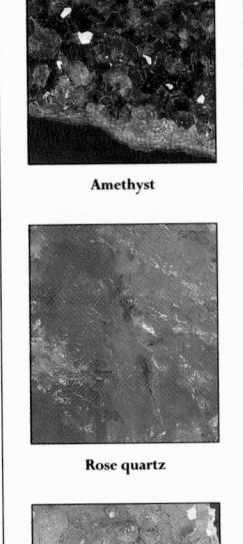

Amethyst

Rose quartz

Citrine

Smoky

Rock crystal

MOHS' HARDNESS: 7.0

SPECIFIC GRAVITY: 2.65–2.66

CRYSTAL SYSTEM: Hexagonal

A GATE SiO₂
SILICATE GROUP

DISTINCTIVE FEATURES Translucent, strongly banded white to grey-blue to orange-red, waxy mineral in rock cavities.

COLOUR Variable: white to grey, whitish-blue, orange to red, grey and black.

LUSTRE Waxy.

STREAK None.

TRANSPARENCY Mostly translucent, but transparent forms occur.

CLEAVAGE None.

FRACTURE Conchoidal, with very sharp edges.

TENACITY Brittle.

FORMS Cryptocrystalline silica filling geodes (*see* Chalcedony).

TWINNING None.

VARIETIES Can grade into opal or chalcedony.

USES Mineral collections.

OCCURRENCE Found filling rock cavities as a secondary mineral deposited by silica-rich water. Often found in metamorphic zones surrounding granite intrusions, but can also occur in sediments. Worldwide.

MOHS' HARDNESS: 7.0

SPECIFIC GRAVITY: 2.6

CRYSTAL SYSTEM: Hexagonal

C HALCEDONY SiO₂
SILICATE GROUP

DISTINCTIVE FEATURES Occurs as waxy, stalactitic, translucent whitish-grey to bluish mineral in rock cavities. Looks rather like candle wax drippings.

COLOUR Variable: clear to white, whitish-blue, grey and black.

LUSTRE Waxy.

STREAK None.

TRANSPARENCY Mostly translucent, but transparent forms occur.

CLEAVAGE None.

FRACTURE Conchoidal, with very sharp edges.

TENACITY Brittle.

FORMS Cryptocrystalline silica in stalactitic and botryoidal forms. Commonly found filling geodes

(*see* Agate).

TWINNING None.

VARIETIES Can grade into opal or agate.

USES Mineral collections.

OCCURRENCE Found filling rock cavities as a secondary mineral deposited by silica-rich water. Often found in metamorphic zones surrounding granite intrusions, but can also occur in sediments. Worldwide.

MOHS' HARDNESS: 7.0

SPECIFIC GRAVITY: 2.6

CRYSTAL SYSTEM: Hexagonal

OPAL SiO_2
SILICATE GROUP

DISTINCTIVE FEATURES No crystal form, pearly to resinous and variously coloured. Gem-quality opals have a distinctive, fiery play of colours that are emphasized when wet.

COLOUR Variable – any colour possible, depending on the type and amount of impurities it contains, but the pure form is white.

LUSTRE Vitreous to subvitreous.

STREAK White.

TRANSPARENCY Normally translucent, but can also be transparent or opaque.

CLEAVAGE None.

FRACTURE Good conchoidal.

TENACITY Brittle.

FORMS Stalactitic, massive as vein fillings, encrusting rocks as small mammillated lumps.

TWINNING None.

VARIETIES Common, which is white or variously coloured, precious, which has a slight play of colours, fire, which is reddish or yellowing with a vivid play of colours, wood, which is petrified wood, and moss, which is opal with dark, tree-like inclusions.

USES Jewellery as a gemstone.

OCCURRENCE Can occur in most rock types as a secondary mineral deposited by silica-rich hot spring waters. Also, in acid igneous rocks as a late stage vein infilling. Common opal is found worldwide, precious opal in "Czechoslovakia", Australia, Mexico, Japan, New Zealand, USA (Wyoming, Nevada).

MOHS' HARDNESS: 7.0

SPECIFIC GRAVITY: 2.3

CRYSTAL SYSTEM: Amorphous

MICROCLINE $KAlSi_3O_8$
SILICATE GROUP

DISTINCTIVE FEATURES Pale turquoise to white, slightly streaked crystals. Similar to orthoclase in appearance, but with slightly lower specific gravity.

COLOUR Pale turquoise to whitish-yellow, sometimes pale brick red.

LUSTRE Vitreous.

STREAK No colour.

TRANSPARENCY Usually translucent, rarely transparent.

CLEAVAGE Perfect on 001.

FRACTURE Uneven.

TENACITY Brittle.

FORMS Prismatic orthorhombic (like orthoclase), also massive to granular.

TWINNING On 100 and 010.

VARIETIES None.

USES Jewellery, ornamental, in porcelain manufacture.

OCCURRENCE Abundant in acid igneous rocks, such as granite. Good crystals may be obtained from granite pegmatites. Worldwide, but particularly the Urals in Russia, Italy, Scandinavia, Madagascar, USA (Pennsylvania, Delaware, Colorado).

MOHS' HARDNESS: 6.0

SPECIFIC GRAVITY: 2.55

CRYSTAL SYSTEM: Triclinic

ORTHOCLASE

KAlSi₃O₈
SILICATE GROUP

DISTINCTIVE FEATURES Speckled, creamy white typical crystal form and two cleavages at 90 degrees.
COLOUR White to mostly creamy white. Often pinkish-red.
LUSTRE Vitreous to pearly.
STREAK No colour.
TRANSPARENCY Mostly subtransparent, rarely transparent.
CLEAVAGE Perfect on 001, good on 010.
FRACTURE Uneven.
TENACITY Brittle.
FORMS Prismatic orthorhombic, twins common. Also massive, granular and cryptocrystalline.
TWINNING On 100 and 010.

VARIETIES Adularia, which is a transparent form, and sanidine, which is a glassy, high-temperature form common in acid lavas.
USES In the manufacture of porcelain, jewellery.
OCCURRENCE Abundant and important rock-forming mineral of acid igneous rocks, schists and gneisses. Good crystals occur in granitic pegmatites. Worldwide, but particularly in Switzerland, Italy, France, UK, Madagascar, Ceylon, USA (New England, Pennsylvania, Arkansas, Colorado, Texas, Nevada and California).

MOHS' HARDNESS: 6.0

SPECIFIC GRAVITY: 2.57

CRYSTAL SYSTEM: Monoclinic

ADULARIA *KAlSi₃O₈*
SILICATE GROUP

DISTINCTIVE FEATURES Bladed to prismatic, white to transparent crystals with a pearly appearance. Occurs in crystalline schists.
COLOUR Clear to white.
LUSTRE Pearly.
STREAK White.
TRANSPARENCY Transparent to translucent.
CLEAVAGE Perfect on 001, good on 010.
FRACTURE Uneven.
TENACITY Brittle.
FORMS Bladed to prismatic crystals with elongated 110 faces.
TWINNING Fairly common on 021.
VARIETIES None.
USES Mineral collections.

OCCURRENCE Adularia is the purest form of orthoclase found in granites, granitic gneisses and schists. It occurs in open druses and pegmatite veins, where it is associated with other granite minerals. Switzerland, Austria, Italy.

MOHS' HARDNESS: 6.0

SPECIFIC GRAVITY: 2.56

CRYSTAL SYSTEM: Monoclinic

PLAGIOCLASE NaAlSi₃O₈ to CaAl₂Si₂O₈

SILICATE GROUP

DISTINCTIVE FEATURES White to grey rhombic to tabular crystals in which the polysynthetic twinning may show as fine parallel striations on crystal faces. Present in almost all igneous and metamorphic rocks.

COLOUR White to greyish-blue or reddish.

LUSTRE Vitreous to pearly.

STREAK No colour.

TRANSPARENCY Mostly translucent, but some forms are transparent.

CLEAVAGE On 001 and 010 at 90 degrees.

FRACTURE Uneven.

TENACITY Brittle.

FORMS Tabular.

TWINNING Polysynthetic twins are common.

VARIETIES Albite, oligoclase, andesine, labradorite, bytownite and anorthite. A continuous compositional series from sodium-rich albite to calcium anorthite in which varieties can be distinguished only by specialized testing.

USES In porcelain manufacture, jewellery.

OCCURRENCE Abundant and important rock-forming mineral of nearly all igneous rocks, but good crystals are only found in pegmatites and similar cavities and veins. Worldwide.

MOHS' HARDNESS: 6.0

SPECIFIC GRAVITY: 2.6–2.7

CRYSTAL SYSTEM: Triclinic

LABRADORITE NaAlSi₃O₈ 30 to 50 per cent CaAl₂Si₂O₈ 70 to 50 per cent

SILICATE GROUP

DISTINCTIVE FEATURES Shows distinct play of bluish colours (chatoyancy) in reflected light due to fine polysynthetic twinning, which causes interference bands to occur.

COLOURS Medium to dull grey.

LUSTRE Satin to pearly.

STREAK No colour.

TRANSPARENCY Translucent to subtransparent.

CLEAVAGE Perfect on 001.

FRACTURE Uneven, sometimes conchoidal.

TENACITY Brittle.

FORMS Mostly granular with large crystals.

TWINNING Lamellar polysynthetic twinning on 010.

VARIETIES A member of the continuous series in the plagioclase feldspars.

USES Ornamental masonry when it occurs as a monominerallic rock.

OCCURRENCE Mostly in basic to intermediate igneous rocks, such as diorite, gabbro, andesite and basalt. Associated with augite and hornblende. Worldwide, but particularly in Scandinavia, Greenland, Italy, Romania, USA (New York), Canada (Labrador, Ontario, Quebec).

MOHS' HARDNESS: 6.3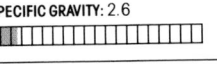

SPECIFIC GRAVITY: 2.6

CRYSTAL SYSTEM: Triclinic

$SODALITE$ $Na_8(Al_6Si_6O_2)Cl_4$
SILICATE GROUP

DISTINCTIVE FEATURES Usually found as lavender blue, dodecahedral crystals or masses in phonolitic lavas.
COLOUR Lavender blue to greenish-yellow.
LUSTRE Vitreous.
STREAK No colour.
TRANSPARENCY Transparent to translucent.
CLEAVAGE Parallel to dodecahedral faces.
FRACTURE Uneven, sometimes conchoidal.
TENACITY Brittle.
FORMS Dodecahedral crystals.
TWINNING None.
VARIETIES None.

USES Mineral collections.
OCCURRENCE In intermediate, fine-grained igneous rocks, such as phonolites. Austria, Italy, Norway, Greenland, USA (Maine, Massachusetts), Canada (Quebec, British Columbia).

MOHS' HARDNESS: 5.5–6.0

SPECIFIC GRAVITY: 2.3

CRYSTAL SYSTEM: Cubic

$LAZURITE$ $(Na,Ca)_{4-8}(Al_6Si_6O_{24}).(SO_4,S)_{1-2}$
SILICATE GROUP

DISTINCTIVE FEATURES Rich Berlin blue dodecahedral (rare) crystals to massive forms. Mostly found in contact metamorphic zones and granite intrusions.
COLOUR Rich Berlin to cerulean blue.
LUSTRE Vitreous.
STREAK Blue.
TRANSPARENCY Translucent.
CLEAVAGE Parallel to crystal faces – poor.
FRACTURE Uneven.
TENACITY Brittle.
FORMS Rare dodecahedral crystals and cubes – mostly occurs in massive form.
TWINNING None.
VARIETIES Synonymous forms are lapis

lazuli and hauynite.
USES Jewellery, mosaics, paint.
OCCURRENCE In limestone affected by contact metamorphism by granite intrusions. In Russia, Afghanistan, Iran, Chile.

MOHS' HARDNESS: 5.0–5.6

SPECIFIC GRAVITY: 2.3–2.4

CRYSTAL SYSTEM: Cubic

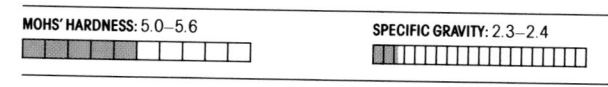

LEUCITE KAlSi₂O₆
SILICATE GROUP

DISTINCTIVE FEATURES Distinctive trapezohedral crystals in recent lavas of trachytic to phonolitic composition. Some crystals fluoresce under ultraviolet light.

COLOUR White to ash-white.

LUSTRE Vitreous to dull.

STREAK No colour.

TRANSPARENCY Usually opaque, sometimes translucent.

CLEAVAGE Poor on 110.

FRACTURE Conchoidal.

TENACITY Brittle.

FORMS Trapezohedral crystals.

TWINNING None.

VARIETIES None.

USES Mineral collections.

OCCURRENCE In potassium-rich, silica-poor, igneous lavas, such as syenites and trachytes. Worldwide, but particularly in Italy, USA (New Jersey, Arkansas, Wyoming), Canada (British Columbia).

MOHS' HARDNESS: 5.0–5.6

SPECIFIC GRAVITY: 2.5

CRYSTAL SYSTEM: Cubic

STILBITE (Ca,Na₂,K₂)Al₂Si₇O₁₈·7H₂O
SILICATE GROUP

DISTINCTIVE FEATURES Waisted, tabular, white crystals filling cracks or lining cavities in basaltic lavas.

COLOUR White to brownish-red.

LUSTRE Vitreous to silky.

STREAK No colour.

TRANSPARENCY Transparent to translucent.

CLEAVAGE Perfect on 010.

FRACTURE Uneven.

TENACITY Brittle.

FORMS Tabular crystals compounded into sheaflike aggregates, giving them a waisted appearance.

TWINNING Often on 001, sometimes interpenetrant or cruciform.

VARIETIES None.

USES Mineral collections.

OCCURRENCE Filling or lining cracks or cavities in basaltic lavas. Iceland, UK, India, Canada (Nova Scotia), USA (New Jersey).

MOHS' HARDNESS: 3.5–4.0

SPECIFIC GRAVITY: 2.0

CRYSTAL SYSTEM: Monoclinic

ROCKS

....

IDENTIFYING ROCKS

Rocks, essentially, are "collections" of different minerals in solid form, although some consist of just one mineral, such as limestone and sandstone. There are three types of rocks: Sedimentary, Igneous and Metamorphic.

Sedimentary rocks are generally stratified, fine-grained or composed of fragments of older rocks from which these were derived, such as pebbles, sand, angular fragments of older rocks, broken shells, rounded mineral grains and altera-

Igneous rocks, such as granite, are usually coarse-grained.

tion minerals such as clays. Limestones are easily identified because they effervesce in dilute hydrochloric acid. Many sedimentary rocks also contain fossils. Igneous rocks, on the other hand, are non-stratified

intrusions or extrusions. They can be extremely coarse-grained (granite), fine (andesite) or glassy (obsidian). They are composed of minerals that have crystallized from molten rock.

Metamorphic rocks are sedimentary or igneous rocks that have been altered by heat and/or pressure. As they are derived from previously existing igneous, sedimentary or even metamorphic rock, their appearance is variable. They are identified by the types of minerals they contain and their texture. Thermally metamorphosed rocks occur bordering igneous intrusions, which altered the surrounding rock originally because of their intense heat, resulting also in the formation of new minerals, such as andalusite and garnet. Regionally metamorphosed rocks occur in the roots of mountain ranges, where intense pressures and high temperatures formed platy minerals (eg micas) and high-pressure minerals (eg staurolite).

PHYSICAL PROPERTIES OF ROCKS

Field specimens of rocks are identified according to their composition, texture and mode of origin. Each major rock type has its own range of textures. Sedimentary rock textures are as follows:

Clastic: Consisting of broken and weathered fragments of pre-existing rocks and/or minerals and/or shell fragments, clastic rocks may have their individual components cemented together by calcite, iron oxide, etc.

Crystalline: Consisting of crystals that have been precipitated from solution, which are locked together like the pieces of a three-dimensional jigsaw puzzle, thus giving the rock great strength without cementing material (eg limestone)

Organic: Mainly composed of well-preserved organic debris, such as plants, shells or bones (eg coal, shelly limestone)

For igneous rocks, the following descriptive terms are used:

Granular: Consisting of crystal grains that are large enough to be easily seen by the naked eye, the grains varying in size from ½ mm in andesites to over 5 mm in granites

Aphanitic: Made up of tiny crystals, which can only be identified using a microscope or powerful hand lens, they give the rock a flow texture (eg basalt) when they are aligned

Glassy: Composed of volcanic glass, sometimes the glass may be streaky, due to aphanitic bands, and may often contain micro crystals of feldspar (eg obsidian)

Pyroclastic: These are volcanic rocks in which the magma has been shattered by an explosive eruption and so may consist of tiny slivers of volcanic glass, fragments of pumice, crystals or fractured rock; they may be unconsolidated or cemented together when fresh and altered to clays by weathering when not (eg tuff, ignimbrite)

Porphyritic: Larger crystals – phenocrysts – are embedded in a finer ground mass; some of the large crystals best being described as megacrysts that have grown in nearly solid rock by means of the replacement of other minerals – a common feature in many granites

Foliated: Minerals are arranged in parallel bands, sometimes contorted as a result of the way the rock flowed while it was still hot and plastic (eg flow-banded rhyolite)

Sandstone is a medium-grained clastic sedimentary rock with grains cemented by iron oxide.

– I D E N T I F I C A T I O N T A B L E F O R I G N E O U S R O C K S –							
TEXTURE	ORTHOCLASE		P L A G I O C L A S E				NO FELDSPAR
	+quartz	−quartz	+quartz	−quartz	pyroxene		+olivine
	+mica	+leucite nepheline	−biotite and/or hornblende		−olivine	+olivine	
GRANULAR	granite	syenite	grano-diorite	diorite	gabbro	olivine gabbro	picrite peridotite
FINELY GRANULAR	micro-granite	porphyry			dolerite	olivine dolerite	
APHANITIC	rhyolite	trachyte phonolite	dacite	andesite	basalt	olivine basalt	
GLASSY	obsidian (massive) pumice (frothy glass) pitchstone (bituminous)		glass		tachylite (like obsidian but not translucent)		
PYROCLASTIC volcanic deposits	ash (unconsolidated air-falls ⅙ in [<4 mm]), volcanic bombs tuff (consolidated air-falls/ash flows ⅙ in [<4 mm]) breccia (angular rock fragments ⅙ in [>4 mm])						

NOTE – gradations may occur between all types.

The following terms are used to describe metamorphic rocks:

Slaty: Finely crystalline rock in which minerals, such as mica, are aligned parallel to one another, which means that the rock splits readily along the mica cleavage planes (eg slate)

Schistose: Minerals, such as mica, chlorite and hornblende, are aligned in easily visible parallel bands and, because of their platy alignment, the rock splits easily (eg schist)

Gneissose: Characterized by a coarse foliation with individual bands up to a few inches (several centimetres) across – indeed, the foliation may wrap around larger crystals, as in Augen gneiss – and all the minerals are coarsely granular and readily identifiable (eg gneiss)

Granoblastic: Mainly large mineral grains that have crystallized at the same time and, therefore, penetrate each other, the grains remaining large enough to be identified easily (eg grauwacke or greywacke)

Hornfels: Compact, finely grained rock that shatters into sharply angular fragments (eg hornfels)

Banded: Components occur in well-defined bands (eg gneiss)

– IDENTIFICATION TABLE FOR METAMORPHIC ROCKS –

MOSTLY FOLIATED (banded or layered structure)			
TEXTURE	NAME	COMPOSITION	DERIVED FROM
SLATY	slate	mica and quartz	shale, tuff
SCHISTOSE	chlorite schist	chlorite, plagioclase, epidote	tuff, andesite, basalt
	mica schist	musocovite, biotite, quartz	shale, tuff, rhyolite
	garnet mica schist	muscovite, biotite, quartz and garnet	shale, tuff, rich in calcium
GNEISSOSE	gneiss	feldspar, quartz, mica, amphibole, occasionally occurring garnet	melting of granitic or sedimentary rocks
BANDED	migmatite	feldspar, quartz, biotite and amphibole	acid and basic rocks
NON-FOLIATED (or slightly foliated)			
TEXTURE	NAME	COMPOSITION	DERIVED FROM
HORNFELSIC	hornfels	dependent on the original rock	sedimentary rocks of fine grain
GRANOBLASTIC	quartzite	quartz	sandstone
	marble (R)*	calcite, calcium and magnesium silicates	limestone or dolomite
	amphibolite	hornblende, plagioclase, quartz, garnet	basic igneous rocks

(R) – reacts with HCl

– ROCK IDENTIFIER SYMBOLS –
The symbols that accompany each rock in the Identifier Section are common symbols used to represent the rock-type on a geological diagram or map.

ROCK IDENTIFIER

CONGLOMERATE
SEDIMENTARY ROCK

DISTINCTIVE FEATURES Boulders, pebbles or shingle, set in fine-grained matrix, sometimes resembling coarse concrete.

COLOUR Variable, depending on the type of rock fragments.

TEXTURE AND GRANULARITY Variable.

COMPOSITION Rounded rock fragments set in a fine-grained matrix.

FIELD ASSOCIATIONS Derived from beach, lake and river deposits of boulders, pebbles and gravel. Often found near deposits of sandstone and arkose.

VARIETIES None.

USES Aggregate, ornamental when highly compacted forms are cut and polished.

OCCURRENCE Worldwide.

BRECCIA
SEDIMENTARY ROCK

DISTINCTIVE FEATURES Similar to conglomerate, but rock fragments are angular and set in fine-grained matrix. Distinguished from agglomerate (volcanic equivalent) by its sedimentary origin.

COLOUR Variable, depending on type of rock fragments.

TEXTURE AND GRANULARITY Angular fragments of rock set in fine-grained matrix.

COMPOSITION Fragmented rocks of any kind can form breccia. The matrix is normally fine sand or silt, cemented by secondary silica or calcite.

FIELD ASSOCIATIONS Derived from screes and fault zones. Often found near conglomerate, arkose and sandstone.

VARIETIES Named according to rock type of which it is composed.

USES Aggregate, ornamental when highly compacted.

OCCURRENCE Worldwide.

SANDSTONE
SEDIMENTARY ROCK

DISTINCTIVE FEATURES Sand in which the grains are cemented together by secondary silica or calcite. May be loosely cemented and soft or well cemented and hard.

COLOUR Buff to brownish; sometimes reddish, due to presence of iron oxides, or greenish, due to presence of glauconite.

TEXTURE AND GRANULARITY Sandy, with grains 2 to 0.06 mm in diameter.

COMPOSITION Sand grains (quartz), cemented by secondary silica or calcite.

FIELD ASSOCIATIONS Compacted and/or cemented ancient beach, river, delta, lake and desert deposits. Occurs as thick, stratified beds in sedimentary sequences, often showing current or dune bedding.

VARIETIES Quartz sandstone, which has cemented rounded or angular quartz grains, greywacke (*see* Greywacke), arkose, which is feldspar-rich sandstone, and calcareous sandstone, which has a high proportion of calcite, usually as cement.

USES Construction industry.

OCCURRENCE Worldwide.

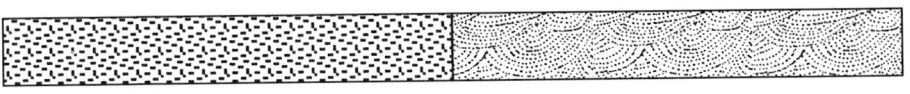

ARKOSE
SEDIMENTARY ROCK

DISTINCTIVE FEATURES Sandstone-rich in feldspars. Bedding is sometimes present, but fossils are rare. It effervesces slightly in dilute hydrochloric acid, which indicates calcite cement.

COLOUR Buff to brownish-grey or pink.

TEXTURE AND GRANULARITY Usually medium-grained (2 mm on average), but can be fine-grained (2 mm to 0.06 mm). Mineral grains do not interlock.

COMPOSITION Quartz sandstone containing over quarter feldspar with calcite or iron oxide cement. Micas may also be present.

FIELD ASSOCIATIONS Derived from rapid weathering, transportation and deposition of granitic rocks.

VARIETIES None.

USES Building stone, millstones for grinding corn.

OCCURRENCE Worldwide.

GREYWACKE
SEDIMENTARY ROCK

DISTINCTIVE FEATURES Poorly sorted dark grey to greenish, fine-grained sandstone.

COLOUR Various shades of dark grey to dark greenish-grey.

TEXTURE AND GRANULARITY Granular, fine-grained.

COMPOSITION Quartz, plagioclase and tiny rock fragments set in a matrix of microscopic quartz, feldspar, clay and other minerals that are too small to determine without a microscope.

FIELD ASSOCIATIONS Formed at bottom of ocean trenches bordering continents by avalanches of submarine sediments. Occurs in association with black shales of deep sea origin.

VARIETIES Feldspathic greywacke, which is rich in feldspar, and lithic greywacke, which is rich in tiny rock fragments.

USES None of any importance.

OCCURRENCE Worldwide, but especially bordering ancient fold mountain ranges.

SHALE
SEDIMENTARY ROCK

DISTINCTIVE FEATURES Splits easily into thin plates along well-defined planes parallel to the original stratification. Buff to grey very fine-grained silty rock.

COLOUR Buff to various shades of grey.

TEXTURE AND GRANULARITY Fine-grained (< -06 mm).

COMPOSITION Complex mixture of microscopic clay minerals, plus mica and quartz.

FIELD ASSOCIATIONS Derived from ancient mud deposits, it occurs in most sedimentary sequences with fine sandstone and limestone.

VARIETIES Probably mudstone.

USES Source of fossils.

OCCURRENCE Worldwide.

LIMESTONE
SEDIMENTARY ROCK

DISTINCTIVE FEATURES Whitish compact rock that effervesces in dilute hydrochloric acid. Often rich in fossils.
COLOUR White to yellowish or grey. Black varieties are rich in hydrocarbons.
TEXTURE AND GRANULARITY Variable: compact, oolitic, crystalline, earthy-granular, pisolitic, shelly.

COMPOSITION Mostly calcium carbonate.
FIELD ASSOCIATIONS Deposited in ancient seas by precipitation or by the accumulation of calcite-rich shells etc, coral reefs, around hot springs.
VARIETIES Crystalline limestone, which has granoblastic calcium carbonate crystals, crinoidal limestone, which is

rich in fragments of fossil crinoids, oolitic limestone, which has tiny ooliths of calcium carbonate, pisolite, which has large (up to 4 mm) ooliths, and reef limestone, which is rich in coral reef fossils.
USES Source of cement, building construction (locally), blackboard chalk.
OCCURRENCE Worldwide.

CHALK
SEDIMENTARY ROCK

DISTINCTIVE FEATURES White, porous rock that effervesces in dilute hydrochloric acid. Often contains bands of flint nodules and is rich in fossils.
COLOUR White to yellowish or grey.
TEXTURE AND GRANULARITY Fine-grained, earthy, crumbly, porous rock.
COMPOSITION Mostly calcium carbonate, with minor amounts of fine silt. Often contains flint and pyrite nodules.
FIELD ASSOCIATIONS Deposited in ancient seas by the accumulation of tests (tiny shells) of microscopic marine orgnisms.
VARIETIES None.
USES As a source of cement.
OCCURRENCE UK, France, Denmark.

SHELLY LIMESTONE

SEDIMENTARY ROCK

DISTINCTIVE FEATURES Pale grey highly fossiliferous rock. Effervesces in dilute hydrochloric acid (care!).

COLOUR Greyish-white to buff or yellowish-grey.

TEXTURE AND GRANULARITY Shelly.

COMPOSITION Mostly entire and broken fossilized shells cemented by calcium carbonate.

FIELD ASSOCIATIONS Represents a thick accumulation of marine shells and other calcite-rich organisms deposited in shallow water.

VARIETIES None.

USES Source of fossils.

OCCURRENCE Worldwide.

DOLOMITE

SEDIMENTARY ROCK

DISTINCTIVE FEATURES Pale-coloured massive limestone that often contains small cavities. Sometimes associated with evaporite deposits of gypsum and halite.

COLOUR Creamy white to pale brown.

TEXTURE AND GRANULARITY Coarse- to fine-grained. Often compact.

COMPOSITION Magnesium carbonate with, at times, small amounts of silica and other derived minerals.

FIELD ASSOCIATIONS Often interbedded with calcite-rich limestones, but may form thick massive deposits.

VARIETIES Sometimes known as magnesium limestone.

USES Aggregate.

OCCURRENCE Worldwide.

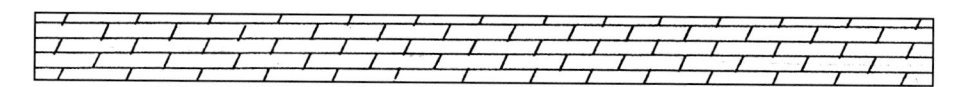

COAL
SEDIMENTARY ROCK

DISTINCTIVE FEATURES Black, dirty, hard to crumbly rock. Burns with a bright yellow flame.

COLOUR Dull, earthy black to glistening submetallic black.

TEXTURE AND GRANULARITY Massive, brittle.

COMPOSITION Highly compacted plant debris.

FIELD ASSOCIATIONS Represents remains of ancient forests that flourished, mainly, on tropical deltas. Occurs mostly as thick beds in rocks of Carboniferous age, although some thin coal bands are found in rocks of other ages.

VARIETIES Cannel coal, which is a soft brownish-black, coal, which is brittle, black, sometimes with glistening bands, and anthracite, which is brittle, black, glistening.

USES Domestic and industrial fuel.

OCCURRENCE USA (Pennsylvania), southern Russia, Ukraine, UK, China, Africa.

SEPTARIAN NODULES
SEDIMENTARY ROCK

DISTINCTIVE FEATURES Ball-like structures, often enclosing shell fragment or other nuclei. Composed of sandstone or clay cemented by calcite or silica, the internal shrinkage cavities, usually filled with calcite, may be seen when the nodule is cut or broken.

COLOUR Variable: grey to buff to dark brown with whitish-yellow calcite filling the interior, radiating cracks and cavities.

TEXTURE AND GRANULARITY Usually fine-grained.

COMPOSITION Variable, depending on origin. Sand, silt or clay together with calcite.

FIELD ASSOCIATIONS Fine-grained or clay sediments.

VARIETIES None.

USES Ornamental when cut and polished.

OCCURRENCE Worldwide.

GRANITE
IGNEOUS ROCK

DISTINCTIVE FEATURES Granular, composed of feldspars and quartz, with accessory biotite and muscovite. One feldspar may be flesh coloured, while the other is white. The white feldspar may show twinning striations characteristic of plagioclase; the other feldspar is almost certainly orthoclase. The quartz appears as grey glassy grains. Biotite is black and muscovite is white or silvery and both shine or sparkle by reflected light.

COLOUR As above.

TEXTURE AND GRANULARITY Granular, coarse-grained, often porphyritic with feldspar crystals up to 4 in (10 cm).

COMPOSITION Orthoclase feldspar is always greater than plagioclase. If plagioclase is dominant the rock is probably a quartz diorite. White to salmon pink orthoclase feldspars megacrysts, set in a ground mass of glassy quartz, white/pink orthoclase, white plagioclase, black biotite and silvery muscovite. Accessory minerals include gold-coloured pyrites and silvery black magnetite.

FIELD ASSOCIATIONS Associated with fold mountains (eg Himalayas and Andes, Urals, Appalachians and Rockies). Granites often mark position of ancient fold mountain systems.

VARIETIES Numerous. Immense variation in granularity and colour — extremely coarse pegmatite, fine-grained microgranite, saccharoidal aplite. Orbicular has composite minerals arranged in ovoid or spherical bodies.

USES Roadstone, building blocks, but has poor resistance to fire as it crumbles when exposed to intense heat.

OCCURRENCE Worldwide.

– VARIETIES –

Pegmatite

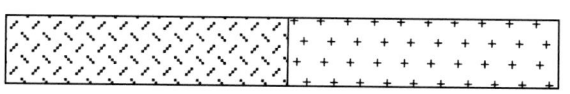

SYENITE
IGNEOUS ROCK

DISTINCTIVE FEATURES Texture and granularity and its composition.

COLOUR White, pinkish-grey to grey.

TEXTURE AND GRANULARITY Granular – coarse to very coarsely grained.

COMPOSITION Orthoclase more dominant than plagioclase (if plagioclase is dominant, the rock is probably diorite). Quartz is absent but there are small amounts of hornblende, mica, augite and magnetite, which are easily seen in coarse examples. Nepheline and leucite may also be present.

FIELD ASSOCIATIONS Uncommon rocks that may be associated with nearby granites, but generally form magma chambers underlying trachytic (the fine-grained equivalent of syenite) volcanoes.

VARIETIES Syenite, which contains more orthoclase than plagioclase and no quartz, nepheline syenite, which has orthoclase and nepheline, and anorthosite, which is mostly plagioclase (labradorite).

USES Building industry, superior to granite because of its fire-resisting qualities.

OCCURRENCE Worldwide, but particularly in the Alps, Germany, Norway, Azores, Africa, Russia, USA (New England, Arkansas, Montana and other states).

GRANODIORITE
IGNEOUS ROCK

DISTINCTIVE FEATURES Texture, colour and the ratio of plagioclase to orthoclase as well as the presence of quartz (polysynthetic twinning sometimes seen as fine striations on plagioclase phenocrysts). Association with granitic masses.

COLOUR Pale to medium grey.

TEXTURE AND GRANULARITY Granular, coarse-grained, often with phenocrysts of feldspar, hornblende or mica.

COMPOSITION More plagioclase than orthoclase, plus quartz. Minor quantities of biotite, hornblende, apatite and sphene are also present.

FIELD ASSOCIATIONS Found in association with granitic batholiths.

Forms large intrusive masses in the roots of mountain ranges.

VARIETIES Hornblende biotite granites, but these are really granodiorites.

USES Roadstone aggregate.

OCCURRENCE Worldwide, but particularly in Scandinavia, Brazil, Canada, USA (California has 3500 square miles [9065 km^2] of granodiorite).

DIORITE
IGNEOUS ROCK

DISTINCTIVE FEATURES Texture and granularity, composition, occurrence.
COLOUR Dark grey, dark greenish-grey to black, depending on the percentage of dark minerals present.
TEXTURE AND GRANULARITY Granular, though not particularly coarse. Hornblende crystals may give it the appearance of a porphyritic texture.
COMPOSITION There is more hornblende than feldspar and more plagioclase than orthoclase. The presence of quartz is uncommon; but, if it is present, the rock is then granodiorite (quartz diorite) rather than diorite.
FIELD ASSOCIATIONS Associated with both granite and gabbro intrusions, into which they may subtly merge.
VARIETIES Granodiorite, when minor amounts of quartz are present.
USES Ornamental – capable of taking a high polish.
OCCURRENCE Worldwide, but particularly in the eroded roots of fold mountains.

+++
+++

GABBRO
IGNEOUS ROCK

DISTINCTIVE FEATURES Colour, granularity, predominance of pyroxene and, often, olivine. May appear to be porphyritic because of the size of the pyroxenes.
COLOUR Dark grey, dark greenish-grey to black.
TEXTURE AND GRANULARITY Coarsely granular, but rarely porphyritic. Sometimes banded, resembling gneiss.
COMPOSITION Mainly pyroxene and plagioclase, with greater amounts of pyroxene than plagioclase or equal amounts of both. Olivine is often present, as well as grains of iron ore (magnetite and/or ilmenite) and bronze-coloured biotite.
FIELD ASSOCIATIONS As plutons and similar large bodies, but not as large as those of granites. Also as large sheets, often containing valuable ore deposits (eg Lake Superior deposits).
VARIETIES Olivine gabbro, which is like gabbro, but also has olivine phenocrysts.
USES Building industry, monumental since it takes a high polish, as a source of iron, nickel and copper ores (eg Sudbury ores in Ontario, Canada).
OCCURRENCE Scotland, Scandinavia, Canada, England, Germany, USA (New England, New York, Minnesota, California and lesser amounts in other states.)

PERIDOTITE (and other ultra basic)
IGNEOUS ROCK

DISTINCTIVE FEATURES Greenish colour when fresh, medium brown when weathered. Texture and composition.

COLOUR Olive green when fresh, but weathering to dark ochre brown due to the formation of iron oxides.

TEXTURE AND GRANULARITY Granular – saccharoidal.

COMPOSITION Made up almost entirely of small grains of olivine, or pyroxene may be present in appreciable amounts.

FIELD ASSOCIATIONS As small intrusions, sills and dykes. Often brought to the surface from a great depth by volcanic activity (olivine nodules in basalt).

VARIETIES Dunite, which is composed of olivine only and is a pistachio green colour, and picrite, which is composed of olivine plus subordinate amounts of plagioclase and is pale green. NOTE: Pyroxenite, which consists only of pyroxene, is black and has a 90 degree cleavage, and hornblendite, which consists only of hornblende, is black and has a 120 degree cleavage.

USES As a source of valuable ores and minerals, including chromite, platinum, nickel and precious garnet. Diamonds are obtained from mica-rich peridotite (kimberlite) in South Africa.

OCCURRENCE Worldwide, but particularly in New Zealand, USA (New York, Kentucky, Georgia, Arkansas, Carolina and lesser amounts in other states).

DOLERITE
IGNEOUS ROCK

DISTINCTIVE FEATURES Colour, texture. Difficult to distinguish between the hornblende and pyroxenes because of their small grain size. The plagioclase occurs as thin laths. Pyrite, bronze biotite and iron oxide may be seen using a hand lens.

COLOUR Medium grey to black.

TEXTURE AND GRANULARITY Granular to fine grains. Occasionally porphyritic.

COMPOSITION Pyroxene and plagioclase with larger amounts of pyroxene than plagioclase or equal amounts of both. Olivine is also often present, as well as grains of iron ore (magnetite and/or ilmenite) and bronze-coloured biotite.

FIELD ASSOCIATIONS As dykes and sills, often of great thickness. It may pass into gabbro at depth (dolerite is the medium-grained equivalent of gabbro).

VARIETIES Olivine dolerite, which is dolerite, plus olivine phenocrysts.

USES Monumental, masonry, paving slabs, aggregate for roadstone.

OCCURRENCE Worldwide, but particularly in Canada (Lake Superior), UK, USA (eastern states – notably Palisades Sill – and western states as lava flows that merge into basalts).

*R*HYOLITE

IGNEOUS ROCK

DISTINCTIVE FEATURES Aphanitic, buff to greyish flow-banded rock, often containing spherulites or phenocrysts of quartz and feldspar.

COLOUR Buff to greyish, banded.

TEXTURE AND GRANULARITY Aphanitic to very fine-grained.

COMPOSITION Same as granite, but the crystals too small to see without using a microscope.

FIELD ASSOCIATIONS As thick lava flows from acidic volcanoes.

VARIETIES Spherulitic rhyolite, which contains rounded bodies (spherules) of microcrystalline quartz and feldspar.

USES Aggregate.

OCCURRENCE Worldwide.

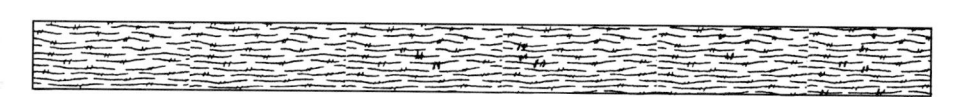

*M*ICROSYENITE

IGNEOUS ROCK

DISTINCTIVE FEATURES Texture and granularity and composition.

COLOUR White to pinkish-grey.

TEXTURE AND GRANULARITY Granular – fine-grained to aphanitic.

COMPOSITION Orthoclase appears in greater quantities than plagioclase and there is no quartz. The small amounts of hornblende, mica, augite and magnetite that are present can only be seen in thin sections with the aid of a microscope. Nepheline and leucite may also be present.

FIELD ASSOCIATIONS This is an uncommon rock, associated with syenite masses.

VARIETIES None.

USES Aggregate.

OCCURRENCE Worldwide, but particularly in the Alps, Germany, Norway, Azores, Africa, Russia, USA (New England, Arkansas, Montana and lesser amounts in other states).

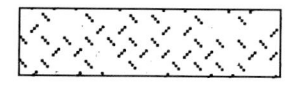

71

A N D E S I T E
IGNEOUS ROCK

DISTINCTIVE FEATURES Colour and texture. Often flow-banded and porphyritic and plagioclase phenocrysts occur as thin laths. Biotite, hornblende and pyroxenes may be seen with the aid of a hand lens, but they can be difficult to identify because they are small.

COLOUR White to black, but mostly medium grey.

TEXTURE AND GRANULARITY Aphanitic to finely granular, porphyritic and flow-banded.

COMPOSITION Fine-grained ground mass of plagioclase, with smaller amounts of hornblende, biotite and augite, which may occur as small phenocrysts.

FIELD ASSOCIATIONS Lava flows and small intrusions associated with volcanic mountain ranges.

VARIETIES Hornblende augite andesite, which is andesite with phenocrysts of hornblende and augite.

USES Roadstone aggregate.

OCCURRENCE Abundant in continental collision zones, such as the Andes, Cascades, Carpathians, Indonesia, Japan and other western Pacific volcanic islands.

B A S A L T
IGNEOUS ROCK

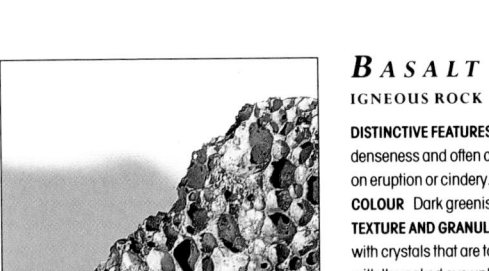

DISTINCTIVE FEATURES Texture, colour, denseness and often contorted by flow on eruption or cindery.

COLOUR Dark greenish-grey to black.

TEXTURE AND GRANULARITY Aphanitic with crystals that are too small to identify with the naked eye unless they occur as phenocrysts (eg augite and/or olivine). Fine-grained equivalent of gabbro.

COMPOSITION Pyroxene and plagioclase, with pyroxene appearing in greater amounts than plagioclase or equal amounts. Olivine is also often present, as well as grains of iron ore (magnetite and/or ilmenite) and bronze-coloured biotite. It may contain olivine or pyroxene nodules brought up from depth.

FIELD ASSOCIATIONS As lava flows, sills and dykes associated with volcanoes.

VARIETIES Olivine basalt, which is basalt plus olivine phenocrysts, and quartz basalt, which is basalt plus scarce quantities of quartz.

USES Roadstone aggregate, source of iron ore, sapphires and native copper.

OCCURRENCE Worldwide, but particularly in Canada (Lake Superior has vast copper deposits), Greenland, India (Deccan traps), Iceland, Scotland, USA (Montana, western states).

OBSIDIAN
IGNEOUS ROCK

DISTINCTIVE FEATURES Black volcanic glass, translucent on fine edges. When opaque on fine edges, the rock is tachylite (basaltic glass).

COLOUR Black, but sometimes Indian red to brown. Has a bright, vitreous lustre on smooth surfaces and is sometimes banded, with spherulites.

TEXTURE AND GRANULARITY Glassy. Breaks with well-defined conchoidal fracture to produce razor sharp slivers of glass, so take care with it.

COMPOSITION Glass with the same chemical composition as granite, syenite or granodiorite. Microscopic crystals of pyroxene may appear as whitish flecks. Microscropic iron ores oxidize to give reddish colours.

FIELD ASSOCIATIONS Associated with volcanic activity as rapidly chilled lava flows.

VARIETIES Pitchstone, which is glass with a bituminous appearance, pumice, which is highly vesiculated glass, and vitrophyre, which is glass with tiny phenocrysts.

USES Primitive tribes use it in the making of cutting tools, arrowheads and spearheads, ornamental.

OCCURRENCE Worldwide, but particularly in Iceland, Hungary, Italy, Lipari, Japan, Scotland, Mexico, New Zealand, Russia, USA (Yellowstone Park,'California, Oregon, Utah, New Mexico, Hawaii).

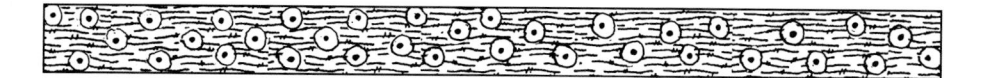

PUMICE
IGNEOUS ROCK

DISTINCTIVE FEATURES White or creamy white highly vesicular rock, but weathers to a pale brown on its surface. Very low density.

COLOUR Creamy white when fresh, but turns pale brown on surface when weathered.

TEXTURE AND GRANULARITY Vesicular.

COMPOSITION Composed principally of glass froth of granitic to granodioritic composition.

FIELD ASSOCIATIONS Chiefly on rhyolitic to dacitic volcanoes.

VARIETIES None.

USES Abrasive, cleansing powders.

OCCURRENCE Worldwide.

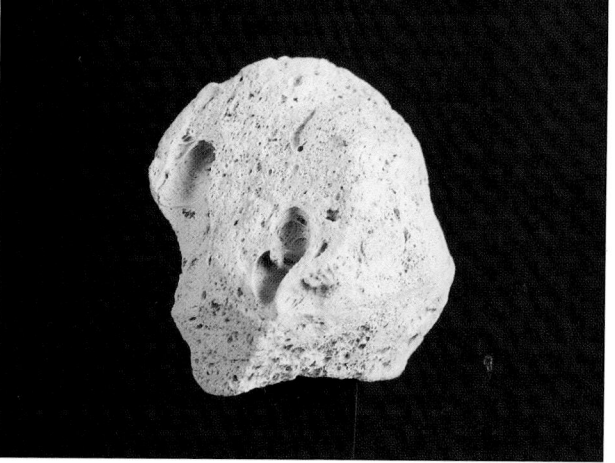

PITCHSTONE
IGNEOUS ROCK

DISTINCTIVE FEATURES Black, opaque volcanic glass that may contain irregular, whitish clusters of minerals. Resembles pitch in appearance.

COLOUR Dull black.

TEXTURE AND GRANULARITY Glassy and breaks to produce poorly defined conchoidal fracture.

COMPOSITION Glass with the same chemical composition as granite, syenite or granodiorite. Microscopic crystals of pyroxene may appear as whitish flecks. Microscopic iron ores oxidize, giving reddish colours.

FIELD ASSOCIATIONS Pitchstone originates from a rapidly chilled lava flow and is therefore always associated with volcanoes.

VARIETIES Obsidian, which is bright black glass with no phenocrysts, pumice, which is highly vesiculated glass, and vitrophyre, which is glass with tiny phenocrysts.

USES Aggregate.

OCCURRENCE Worldwide, but particularly in Iceland, Italy, Lipari, Japan, Mexico, New Zealand, Russia, USA (Yellowstone Park, California, Oregon, Utah, New Mexico, Hawaii and lesser amounts in other states).

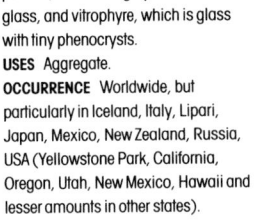

ASH (and related rocks)
IGNEOUS ROCK

DISTINCTIVE FEATURES Unconsolidated or poorly consolidated white to black cindery ash of varying grain size.

COLOUR Variable, ranging from pure white to black.

TEXTURE AND GRANULARITY Pyroclastic. Unconsolidated when fresh, but consolidating to form hard volcanic tuff over geological time.

COMPOSITION Dependent on the composition of the source magma. Mostly basaltic (black) to trachytic (white).

FIELD ASSOCIATIONS As stratified beds of air-fall material ejected by volcanic eruptions, sometimes unstratified when formed from ash flows.

VARIETIES Basaltic ash, which is coarse, cindery to fine black ash, trachytic (syenitic) ash, which is coarse, cindery to fine creamy white ash, and tuff, which is dense, compact rock, varying in colour from cream to yellow.

USES Prefabricated building blocks, road surfacing, abrasives.

OCCURRENCE Worldwide and always associated with volcanoes.

IGNIMBRITE
IGNEOUS ROCK

DISTINCTIVE FEATURES Fine-grained to aphanitic, buff to dark brown compact rock with parallel streaks or lenticles of black glass.

COLOUR Pale cream to brownish to dark red-brown.

TEXTURE AND GRANULARITY Fine-grained to aphanitic and flow foliation is often present.

COMPOSITION Usually trachytic/phonolitic to andesitic.

FIELD ASSOCIATIONS Exclusively produced by violently explosive volcanoes.

VARIETIES Sillar, which is poorly consolidated rock of same origin as ignimbrite but in which pumice blocks have *not* collapsed to form plates of black glass and which is poorly sorted.

USES Local building construction, aggregate.

OCCURRENCE Worldwide – associated with andesitic to phonolitic/trachytic volcanoes.

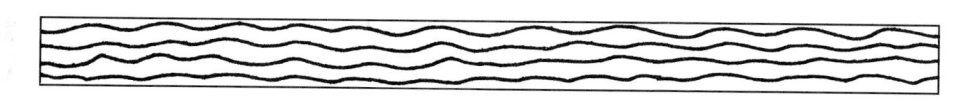

ECLOGITE
IGNEOUS ROCK

DISTINCTIVE FEATURES Generally coarse, green (reddish when weathered) pyroxene in which are set red garnets.

COLOUR Pistachio green when fresh, but mottled with red when weathered.

TEXTURE AND GRANULARITY Granular – coarse- to medium-grained.

COMPOSITION Omphacite (green pyroxene), green hornblende and pyrope-almandine garnet. Kyanite and diamond sometimes occur.

FIELD ASSOCIATIONS Metamorphosed gabbro, or basic magma crystallized at high pressure at great depth.

VARIETIES Coarse- and medium-grained varieties only.

USES Scientific.

OCCURRENCE As blocks in the "blue ground" that fills diamond pipes in Kimberley, South Africa, Norway, Scotland, USA, Asia.

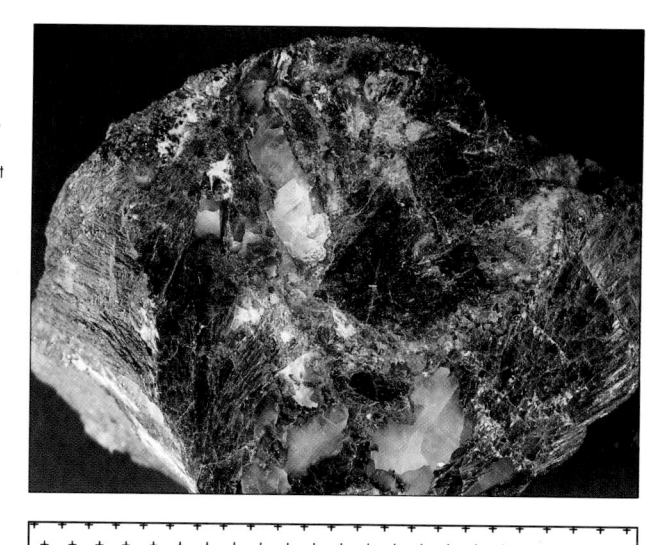

PYROCLASTICS and miscellaneous volcanic products
IGNEOUS ROCK

Thick pumice deposit

VOLCANIC BOMB Rounded or spindle-shaped rock of mainly basaltic composition ejected during eruptions.

BREADCRUST BOMB Rounded, smooth-surfaced pumice block with cracked surface resembling cracked crust of bread, hence the name.

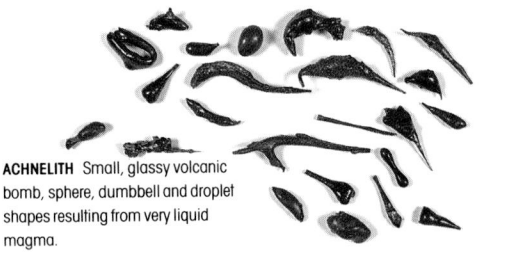

ACHNELITH Small, glassy volcanic bomb, sphere, dumbbell and droplet shapes resulting from very liquid magma.

PAHOEHOE LAVA Vesicular, basaltic lava with ropy surface texture.

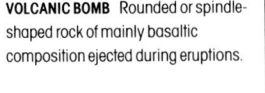

RETICULITE Lightest rock known. A basaltic pumice in which the walls of the vesicles have collapsed, leaving a network of fine, interconnecting glass threads.

PALAGONITE Submarine lava flow altered to yellowish-brown colour by the formation of the gel mineral palagonite.

SLATE
METAMORPHIC ROCK

DISTINCTIVE FEATURES Greyish, very fine-grained, foliated rocks that split into thin sheets. Sometimes contain well-formed pyrite crystals. Found in metamorphic environments.
COLOUR Usually shades of medium to dark grey, but sometimes a buff colour.
TEXTURE AND GRANULARITY Slaty and very fine-grained.
COMPOSITION Mica, quartz and other minerals that can be determined only by x-ray.
FIELD ASSOCIATIONS In areas of regionally metamorphosed shale or volcanic tuff.
VARIETIES None.
USES Roofing sheets.
OCCURRENCE Worldwide.

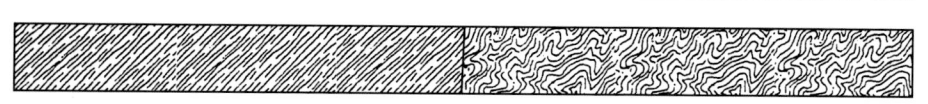

SCHIST
METAMORPHIC ROCK

DISTINCTIVE FEATURES Schistose and mostly composed of biotite, muscovite and quartz. Sometimes contains green chlorite or garnets or staurolite and kyanite.
COLOUR Variable: streaky, silvery, black, white or green.
TEXTURE AND GRANULARITY Schistose with mineral grains that are platy or aligned.
COMPOSITION Mostly muscovite, biotite and quartz but sometimes some green chlorite is present. May also contain large, well-formed crystals of garnet.
FIELD ASSOCIATIONS Zones of contact or regional metamorphism.
VARIETIES Greenschist, which is soft

schist rich in green chlorite, mica schist, which is rich in micas, garnet mica schist, which is mica schist rich in garnets, staurolite-kyanite schist, which is mica schist, rich in these minerals and amphibolite schist, which is mostly amphibole and plagioclase.
USES Source of minerals for collectors.
OCCURRENCE Worldwide, adjacent to large, igneous intrusions or in eroded roots of fold mountain systems.

GNEISS
METAMORPHIC ROCK

DISTINCTIVE FEATURES Coarse-grained, pale-coloured gneissose rock, containing abundant feldspar.

COLOUR Whitish to dark grey – the darker varieties containing more biotite.

TEXTURE AND GRANULARITY Gneissose, coarse-grained.

COMPOSITION Mostly feldspar, with quartz, mica, hornblende and garnet.

FIELD ASSOCIATIONS In roots of eroded fold mountain systems.

VARIETIES Depends on the source rock.

Granitic gneiss is the most common, but basic varieties also occur.

USES Construction, ornamental, aggregate.

OCCURRENCE Worldwide, but always in roots of fold mountain systems.

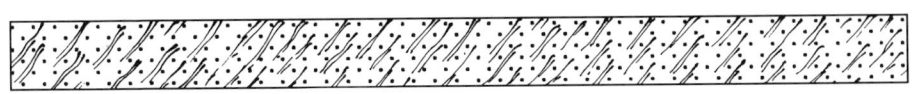

HORNFELS
METAMORPHIC ROCK

DISTINCTIVE FEATURES Hard, compact rock that breaks into splintery fragments. Mineral content is variable. Found in zones of contact metamorphism.

COLOUR Dark to medium grey.

TEXTURE AND GRANULARITY Hornfelsic and fine-grained, sometimes with porphyroblastic crystals.

COMPOSITION Dependent on parent rock.

FIELD ASSOCIATIONS Zone or aureole of contact metamorphism bordering granitic intrusions.

VARIETIES Cordierite hornfels, which contains crystals of cordierite, andalusite hornfels, which contains crystals of andalusite, pyroxene hornfels, which contains crystals of pyroxene, and sillimanite hornfels, which contains crystals of sillimanite.

USES Aggregate.

OCCURRENCE Worldwide.

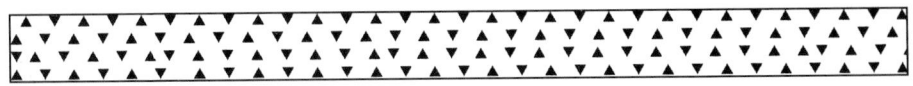

QUARTZITE
METAMORPHIC ROCK

DISTINCTIVE FEATURES Compact, hard, very fine-grained rock, which breaks into sharp angular fragments. Quartzite is always associated with other metamorphic rocks, while cemented sandstone is always associated with other sedimentary rocks.

COLOUR White to creamy white.

TEXTURE AND GRANULARITY Granoblastic and very fine-grained.

COMPOSITION Interlocking sand (quartz) grains, often with silica cement.

FIELD ASSOCIATIONS In zones of regionally metamorphosed sandstones.

VARIETIES Local varieties based on colour.

USES Aggregate, monumental.

OCCURRENCE Worldwide.

MARBLE
METAMORPHIC ROCK

DISTINCTIVE FEATURES Fine- to coarse-grained granoblastic that effervesces in dilute hydrochloric acid. Often banded with various colours and sometimes veined.

COLOUR Variable: white, cream, grey, red, green and often streaky with light and dark patches.

TEXTURE AND GRANULARITY Fine- to coarse-grained, granoblastic.

COMPOSITION Calcium carbonate.

FIELD ASSOCIATIONS In zones of regionally metamorphosed limestone.

VARIETIES Many, depending on the colour and banding, eg Connemara marble, which is pale green.

USES Building and ornamental.

OCCURRENCE Worldwide.

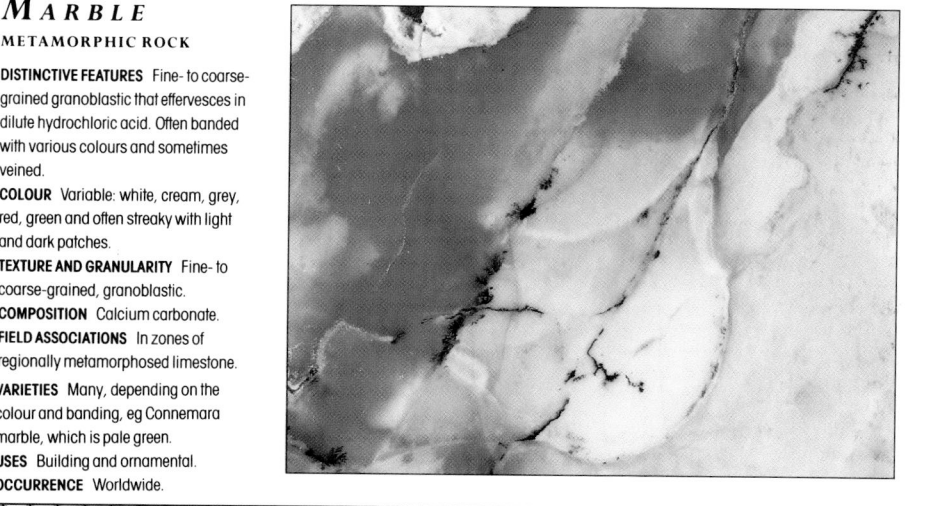

INDEX

....

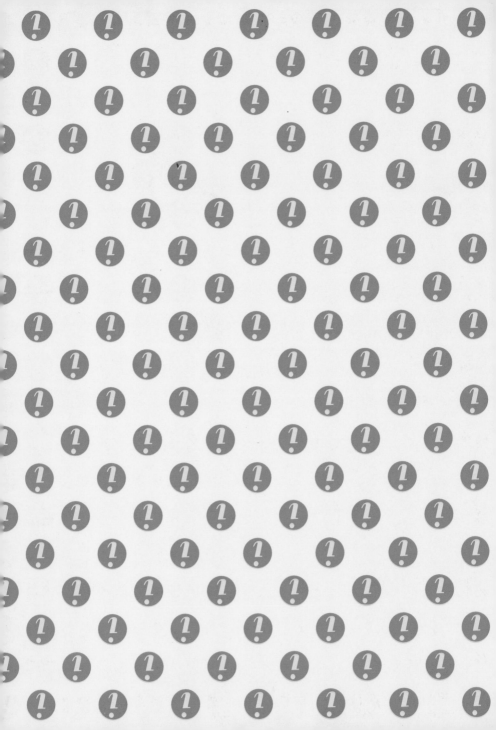